new prairie kitchen

new prairie kitchen

kitchen

Stories and Seasonal Recipes *from* Chefs, Farmers, and Artisans *of the* Great Plains

Summer Miller

PHOTOGRAPHS BY **Dana Damewood**

MIDWAY

AN AGATE IMPRINT

CHICAGO

Printed in China

New Prairie Kitchen
First printing February 2015
Hard cover
ISBN-13: 978-1-57284-167-3
ISBN-10: 1-57284-167-2

Photo on p. 238 by Alison Bickel
Photo on p. 239 by Corrie Suhr
All other photographs copyright © Dana Damewood

Library of Congress Cataloging-in-Publication Data has been applied for.

10 9 8 7 6 5 4 3 2 1   15 16 17 18

Midway Books is an imprint of Agate Publishing. Agate books are available in bulk at discount prices. For more information, go to agatepublishing.com.

For my husband, Steve Widhalm, and our children, Jackson and Juniper.

Contents

Introduction

Through food, we start conversations, settle arguments, and come together in these hectic times. Food is how we celebrate our achievements, comfort the grief stricken, and simply connect to those around us. A meal is both community and communion.

Great Plains states are often referred to as "flyover" country, meaning there aren't many reasons to stop here and look around. These prairie states are typically known for commodity production of corn, soybeans, beef, and pork. Recently, however, a "good food" movement has begun percolating in the region, creating a delicious clash of Old Prairie meets New Prairie, where delicacies such as bison, ground cherries, and sunchokes are used in new and interesting ways. Sure, we still have traditional steak houses in Nebraska—most of which can grill a mean flat iron—and Iowa still raises plenty of commodity pork. But we also have phenomenally talented farmers who grow asparagus thick as your thumb and tender as a strawberry, and chefs who transform it into edible art.

Food is the plate upon which we serve our humanity. A dish is perfectly made not when the spices are balanced or the texture is just right, but when the intention in offering it to another person is pure. I believe such intention can be tasted, that the heart of the cook and the soul of the farmer season the dish. Good food does not have to be pretentious. It can be humble, complex, beautiful, simple, and mouthwatering—and it can come from the minds, hands, and hearts of those in flyover country.

Small local farms and the chefs who support them contribute to our communities through their entrepreneurial spirit, the collaborative nature of their relationships, and the basic act of nourishing others. Skilled farmers know which plants taste better if harvested in cooler weather—broccoli, kale, and brussels sprouts among them. When broccoli has been harvested at the right time and grown in the correct conditions, it's tender and almost sweet, which means my children will eat it and my family will be healthier for it. A tomato that ripens on the vine at the peak of the summer is a great-tasting tomato. It's food worth waiting for, worth savoring, and worth serving to the people I love.

It's food worth waiting for, worth savoring, and worth serving to the people I love.

As a mother and a lover of good food, I have an urgent desire to raise my children with a sense of place; to build up around them a life full of flavor, history, and humility—a life full of people who are inspired by their work and who consider the impact of that work on the greater good.

I come from a family of entrepreneurs. I have seen what it takes to start something, to pour your heart into it, and to risk everything to make it succeed. I admire the grit it takes to build a living from a dream and the integrity required to stay true to your values when times are lean. The best gift we can give ourselves and those we love is an intimate understanding of authentic flavors, people, and places.

New Prairie Kitchen pays homage to the outstanding and innovative chefs, farmers, and artisans of Nebraska, Iowa, and South Dakota. They have shared some of their favorite recipes here, organized by season and focused on regionally sourced meat, poultry, game, and produce. Profiles of these exceptional people are nestled throughout the book.

I set out to learn a little more about what was available within a 200-mile radius of my hometown of Omaha, Nebraska. It turns out quite a bit, but it took some digging. I want buying local food and supporting restaurants that source from local farms to be easier, which is why a resource directory with contact information for every farm, artisan, and restaurant mentioned can be found in the back of this book (p. 226).

As you cook your way through *New Prairie Kitchen* and become acquainted with the tastes and personalities within, you may combine components of one recipe with elements of another to create an entirely new meal. You may find that you prefer the creative and vibrant regional American menus of chef Clayton Chapman from The Grey Plume, or the light, vegetable-laden fare of Maggie Pleskac from Maggie's Vegetarian Cafe. This book offers opportunities for those new to the kitchen as well as challenges for home cooks who consider boeuf bourguignon child's play.

My hope is that *New Prairie Kitchen* will bring your loved ones to the table to share a beautiful meal, but, more importantly, to enjoy one another's company. Ultimately, why we support anything is a personal matter and I would suspect you have your reasons. May *New Prairie Kitchen* help you on your culinary journey, wherever that may lead. ■

Recipe and Ingredient Tips

When cooking from scratch, it can be difficult to predict exact measurements. For example, the ricotta you make might yield four or five cups, but the recipe only calls for three cups. Knowing what to do with leftover ricotta is helpful, which is why I've included some suggestions for what to do with leftover pieces, cups, and tablespoons here.

Braising Liquid

Braising liquid is rich with flavor from the meat and vegetables cooked in it. Think of it like a stock. In most cases, you pour the liquid through a strainer, reduce it, and add it back to the meat. Even still, sometimes there is more liquid than needed, or life gets in the way and you don't have time to reduce it as much as you would've liked. In that case, you can pour leftover braising liquid into an ice cube tray, freeze it, and use one of the individual portions as the base for your next pot of stew. You already did the work—why not keep it and use it to build the flavor profile of your next meal? The same goes for slow-cooker juices: strain the solids and cool the liquid; once it's cold, you can scrape the fat off the top and freeze the liquid.

Cream and Butter

Recipes in this book call for heavy cream and butter. I use these on a regular basis in daily meal planning. You may not, but no worries; they can be frozen and used later without negatively impacting your dish. Remove the cream from the freezer and within a day or two (depending on how much cream you froze) it will be thawed. Shake it vigorously to reincorporate the butterfat and use it as if it were never frozen. For butter, transfer it from the freezer to the refrigerator to use when needed.

If a recipe does not specify whether to use salted or unsalted butter, use unsalted.

Eggs

With farm-fresh eggs, the yolks tend to be a deep, rich orange color, and in lighter-colored desserts they can create a yellowish tint to the finished product. The color shift is subtle, but it's something a baking perfectionist would definitely pick up on. You want that orange yolk; it's a good thing.

Egg whites will keep covered in the refrigerator for three to four days. This comes in handy when making Nick Strawhecker's pappardelle recipe (p. 141), which calls for a yolk-only pasta dough. If you don't plan to use the whites within four days, you can freeze them instead. You can actually freeze the whole egg and the yolks as well, although your approach will differ a bit for each.

For whole eggs, use a fork to mix the white and the yolk together before freezing. For egg whites, just freeze them. No need to do anything else. For the yolks, whisk in 1½ teaspoons of sugar or ⅛ teaspoon of salt for every four yolks before freezing to help maintain the texture or viscosity of the yolks. Ice cube trays work great for freezing eggs. Once frozen, place the egg cubes in a baggie and label them as sweetened or savory yolks, whole eggs, or whites. Don't forget to include the number of yolks or eggs per cube when you transfer them to a baggie. You can use them as you would fresh eggs; just give them 24 hours to thaw in a sealed container in the refrigerator.

Some of the recipes in this book include raw egg. Personally, I feed my family unpasteurized farm-fresh eggs, and I don't worry a bit about letting my kids eat raw cookie dough. That being said, this message is printed on the bottom of most restaurant menus: *consuming raw or*

You want that orange yolk; it's a good thing.

undercooked eggs may increase your chance of foodborne illness, especially if you have a medical condition. So, do what you think is in your best interest when preparing recipes that call for raw eggs or runny yolks.

George Paul Vinegar

Some of the recipes in this book call for George Paul Vinegar; if you don't have it, leave it out. Do not try to replace it with typical grocery store vinegar. George Paul Vinegar is slow-batch vinegar produced in Cody, Nebraska. It's made using Nebraska grapes and is aged between 6 and 18 months, depending on the variety. The aging process concentrates the fruit flavors and aroma. You can purchase it online at www. georgepaulvinegar.com, or, if you live in a larger city, you can find it at specialty food stores.

Meat

When you are ready to venture into using different cuts of meat, sometimes you will need to preorder them from a butcher; other times you're better off purchasing a whole or half animal from a local farmer.

The first step to buying a whole animal is finding a farmer whose product you trust. You can find reputable farmers in the back of this book (p. 226), or at your local farmers' market. Many states and communities have Buy Fresh Buy Local campaigns; they are easy to find if you search the Internet for Buy Fresh Buy Local with the name of your state or city. The second step is contacting the meat processor to provide cutting instructions.

The meat processor is the closest thing we have today to the old-world concept of butchers. A processor receives the live animal, kills it, skins it, eviscerates it, breaks it down into primal cuts, and, from there, transforms it into your dinner. He or she will ask you, "How do you want it?" and you will need to tell him or her. This is typically where the processor hears crickets from your end of the line until he or she helps you understand the anatomy of the animal and your own eating habits.

Depending on the price you're willing to pay, processors cut, grind, cure, smoke, precook, and shred the meat, then package it based on the needs of you and your family. This book has a recipe that calls for a

The meat processor is the closest thing we have today to the old-world concept of butchers.

broken-down whole chicken (p. 35); if you don't want to cut up a whole chicken, ask your processor to do it for you. It's important to understand that you will pay two people: the first is the farmer for the animal, and the second is the processor for the service he or she provides.

Typically, pork and beef should be consumed within 6 to 9 months of purchase, even when stored in a deep freezer; for poultry and rabbit it's about 9 to 12 months. All of it is still edible beyond a year or more, but the flavor will likely be compromised. If you have only the freezer attached to your refrigerator, it is probably best to share the cost of the animal and its meat with a friend or two. Meat is good, but you probably don't want to eat it for every meal. Plus, you will need some room in that freezer for ice cream. At least I do.

The last task is to pick up your meat and stock your freezer. In my house, I have a stand-up deep freezer in my garage currently stuffed with wild pork, deer, two whole chickens, and a few dwindling packages of ground beef from our share of a quarter cow we purchased with some friends.

I use a freezer inventory list to help me keep track of what I have and when I need to use it, which sounds fancier than it really is. The point is to make cooking easier, not harder. It's worth the few minutes it takes to write out a freezer inventory list to help with planning meals. Jot down what you have—sausage, pork chops, bacon, shoulder, hams, loins, whole chicken, whole chicken broken down—and how much, then tape it inside one of your cupboards. When you take an item out of the freezer to use, cross it off the list. When you are changing your lifestyle from multiple trips to the store to multiple trips to your freezer, it's nice to have a plan, especially if you are cooking for a family.

If you'd rather start small and get used to the idea before purchasing a whole or half animal, it's worthwhile to build a relationship with your local meat processor or butcher (who likely works at an independent meat shop). This book uses cuts that can be difficult to find in a conventional supermarket. Specialty stores or small-town processors are more likely to supply the cuts you want.

I realize in urban areas very few people have space for a deep freezer, but if you do, it's one of the most valuable components of home cooking.

Onions

If a recipe doesn't call for a certain type of onion, use yellow onions (or whatever onion you like best).

Pasta

Learning to cook in stages provides you with the best opportunity to eat delicious, whole-food meals at home. In this book, a single pasta recipe will include making the pasta noodles, the tomato sauce, and the sauce base all from scratch. It's a lot to pull together on a weeknight, but if you made the noodles (and even the tomato sauce) last month and froze them, then all you need to do is thaw the pasta, whip up the base, and bring some water to a boil. Fresh pasta takes about 2 minutes to cook, whereas dried pasta from a box can take anywhere from 8 to 15 minutes.

Once you get the hang of making pasta dough from scratch, you can double or triple batches and freeze them as dough rounds, ready-to-go pasta nests, or bags of ravioli. Remove the dough from the freezer in the

morning and it will be ready by dinner. I've thawed it both on the countertop and in the refrigerator.

You will see in this book that different chefs have different pasta dough recipes—some use yolks only, while others use the whole egg. Find the recipe you favor and use that every time if you like. You can use the same dough for ravioli or noodles, and you don't need a pasta machine or attachment. I've made every batch on my countertop with a rolling pin, often with a child at each hip.

Ricotta

Ricotta is a neutral-flavored cheese. You can make it sweet or savory and use it for dinner or dessert. It will keep in the fridge for about five days. You can combine it with herbs, spices, arugula, or spinach to make a fast and simple filling for ravioli, which can then be frozen. You can also fold in almond extract and drizzle with some honey to spread on toast, or serve with baked pears.

Salt

Some recipes specify a type of salt to use (kosher, sea, etc.), while others do not. Where it's not specified, go with your personal preference. Always taste as you go along to prevent oversalting. ■

Spring

Roasted Asparagus Quiche

SERVES 8 (DOUGH YIELDS 1 9-INCH CRUST)

Quiche makes quick work of breakfast, brunch, or lunch. The filling here is more cream than egg. You can make the filling three days ahead of time and store in your refrigerator. The crust can be made months ahead of time and frozen.

—*Kristine Moberg* QUEEN CITY BAKERY | SIOUX FALLS, SD

CRUST

1 cup plus 3 tablespoons all-purpose flour, plus more for rolling dough

½ teaspoon kosher salt

7 tablespoons chilled butter, cubed

3 tablespoons ice water

FILLING

10–12 stalks asparagus

Olive oil, for drizzling

½ teaspoon kosher salt, plus more for asparagus

½ teaspoon ground white pepper, plus more for asparagus

2 eggs

2 egg yolks

1 cup heavy cream

1 cup whole milk

⅛ teaspoon ground nutmeg

⅔ cup grated gruyère cheese or any swiss cheese

WHERE TO FIND...

Asparagus
The Cornucopia
Sioux Center, IA

Dairy
Burbach's Countryside Dairy
Hartington, NE

TO MAKE THE CRUST

In a food processor, combine the flour and salt and pulse a couple of times to mix. Add the butter and pulse until it is in pea-sized pieces. Add the water in a steady stream, stopping twice to scrape the mixture down from the side of the processor.

Lay a sheet of plastic wrap on a flat surface. Turn the dough mixture out onto the plastic wrap. Form the dough into a ball; wrap tightly with the plastic wrap, then press into a fat disc. Chill in the refrigerator for at least 3 hours.

TO MAKE THE FILLING AND PREPARE THE QUICHE

Preheat the oven to 350°F.

Trim the ends off your asparagus stalks if they are woody. Place on a baking sheet, drizzle with the olive oil, and sprinkle with the salt and pepper. Using your hands, gently toss them around a bit to make sure the stalks are evenly coated, and then spread them into a single layer on the baking sheet. Roast for about 15 to 20 minutes. Cool, and then chop into 1-inch pieces. Set aside.

Lightly flour your countertop and roll out the dough, dusting as needed so it doesn't stick. (If it's too difficult to roll out, let it sit at room temperature for 10 minutes or so.) Gently fold the dough into a 9-inch pie plate and form it to the edge of the plate. Prick the bottom of the crust with a fork a few times. Place a sheet of parchment paper on top of the crust and fill it with pie weights. If you don't have weights, just fill the pie shell with dried beans. Bake the shell for 15 minutes, remove from the oven, remove the weights, and then bake for 10 more minutes. It is finished when it looks dry.

While the crust is baking, in a medium bowl, whisk together the eggs and yolks. Gradually add the heavy cream and milk and whisk to incorporate. Whisk in the ½ teaspoon each of salt and pepper as well as the nutmeg.

Once the crust has finished baking, remove it from the oven. Increase the oven temperature to 375°F.

Sprinkle the cheese in the bottom of the baked crust. Top with the asparagus and fill the crust with the egg mixture. Bake for 40 minutes. Let cool at room temperature for about 10 minutes before serving.

Wild Mulberry Vinaigrette

SERVES 8 (2–3 TABLESPOONS PER SERVING)

The mulberry is a pretty humble, unsexy fruit. It's most often associated with purple stains on the driveway, caused by the crush of fallen berries under the tires of the car, or on the fingertips of kids who found a wild treasure trove in the field and ate them straight from the tree limbs. Mulberries do, however, have a place on the table. They uniquely combine subtle sweetness with the musty grassiness of the wild prairie. A bite of a mulberry takes me back to the smell of the fescue grass meadow on my childhood farm in Oklahoma. I love how food can produce this kind of reminiscence. This vinaigrette pairs well with spinach or the peppery leaves of arugula.

—Kevin Shinn BREAD AND CUP | LINCOLN, NE

1½ cups fresh mulberries (to make about ¼ cup strained mulberry juice)

¾ cup canola oil

¼ cup rice wine vinegar

2 tablespoons honey

Pinch salt

WHERE TO FIND…

Mulberries
Any Roadside and Most Backyards
NE

Honey
Sanders Specialty Meats
and Produce
Dwight, NE

To obtain the mulberry juice, you can mechanically extract the mulberry juice in a juicer, or you can manually crush the mulberries in a bowl and strain the juice through a fine-mesh strainer or cheesecloth. Discard the solids.

In a blender, combine the ingredients until completely emulsified (until the oil has combined with the liquid). Serve right away. The vinaigrette will separate after a few minutes; just shake or whisk it vigorously before serving again.

Notes: As with all recipes, adjustments may be necessary. Put more honey if you want it sweeter, less if you like it tarter. If you need to make a larger quantity, just keep the basic oil-to-vinegar ratio at 3 to 1.

If you are using this dressing for a salad that has some type of meat in it, it's best to dress your greens first and then top with your preferred protein. The purple color is prominent, and pouring a purple streak across your sliced chicken breast doesn't always look appetizing.

The Musser Family

ARTISANS MILTON CREAMERY | MILTON, IA | WWW.MILTONCREAMERY.COM

Milton Creamery sits alongside a forgotten highway in a town of fewer than 500 people. Women wearing bonnets and driving buggies brace themselves against the spring rain while the royal-blue undersides of their capes flap and curl in the wind. Rolling hills, windmills, and wandering cows complete the community's bucolic image and solidify the feeling that I've traveled back in time.

Inside an ivory-and-green steel building, Rufus Musser III stands behind a counter full of squeaky cheese curds, waiting to greet hungry, road-weary travelers.

"Welcome," Rufus says in a thick Pennsylvania Dutch accent, with a smile that stretches from one ear to the other. His small, five-foot-six-inch frame practically shudders with enthusiasm. His eyes invite my response and seem to eagerly await bits of small talk. He pauses for a second. We look at one another; then his arms leave their post at his hips to make a big sweeping motion. "Follow me," he says, and we disappear behind the blue swinging doors of the cheese plant, where I am immediately overwhelmed by the scent of pine.

In 1992, Rufus moved to the town of Milton with his wife, Jane. They wanted to farm, but the cost of land where they lived on the East Coast was too high. Iowa, however, was still recovering from the farm crisis of the 1980s, which meant land was available at a price they could afford. Better still, Milton is home to a small Mennonite community, which provided an established way of life for the Mussers while they built a family and business of their own.

"I didn't consider myself a farmer, but it's what I grew up with and it's what I knew. The wife really thought milking cows would be cool, so I promised her I would milk cows until I found something better to do. How's that for being wacky?" Rufus says with a shoulder shrug and a chuckle.

"The wife really thought milking cows would be cool, so I promised her I would milk cows until I found something better to do."

Today, his 24-year-old son, Galen, is the head cheesemaker, and has been since the age of 16. His youngest son, Mark, hauls in milk from a dozen neighboring Amish dairy farms, all of which maintain pastured herds of fewer than 70 cows. His eldest son, Rufus Musser IV, who goes by Junior, acts as the general manager, and Jane is the friendly voice on the phone taking orders and answering questions. Rufus, who is clearly the effervescent socialite of the family, happily gave up milking cows and managing cattle to sell cheese, meet people, and market the creamery at food demonstrations across the country—a role that feels like home to him.

As we near the aging rooms, the scent of pine intensifies with every step. Finally, we turn the corner to find soft aromatic wood boxes stacked 16 high and 14 rows deep. Each box holds roughly 40 pounds of Prairie Breeze, a mild, sweet, aged cheddar with bits of calcium crunch. It's one of Milton Creamery's most decorated and popular cheeses.

True to the Mussers' Mennonite values of simplicity, ingenuity, and hard work, the boxes are simply a functional and affordable way to age cheese. They eliminate the need for shelves and maximize storage space. Across the hall, and inside traditional aging caves full of wood shelves, the lighthearted personas of Galen and his father are replaced with concentration and methodology. The men work like cogs in a clock, turning truckles, which are 20-pound cylinders of clothbound cheddar

made by a neighboring Amish family. The truckles are brought to Milton to mature for 12 to 16 months before they're shipped throughout the country. Soon the job is complete, and Rufus's jovial nature has returned as he guides me back toward the front of the plant.

"You know," Rufus says just before handing me a bag full of aged cheddars; Quark, a fresh European-style cheese; and curds. He has a smile on face. "There are only three things that get better with age—wine, cheese, and women." ∎

Spring Salad with Egg, Bacon, and Fingerling Potatoes

SERVES 4

This is my favorite salad. I was inspired by a meal I had in a little café in Champagne, France. When I tasted it I knew I wanted to come back home and make a similar salad for one of my restaurants using local ingredients. It's suitable for breakfast, lunch, or dinner.

—*George Formaro* CENTRO | DES MOINES, IA

DRESSING

½ cup olive oil

2 tablespoons white wine or champagne vinegar

1 tablespoon Dijon mustard

¾ teaspoon salt

½ teaspoon minced garlic

Big pinch freshly ground black pepper

Pinch granulated sugar

SALAD

8 slices bacon

½ pound fingerling potatoes or assorted small potatoes, sliced ¼ inch thick

Salt and freshly ground black pepper, to taste

2 tablespoons salted butter

4 eggs

8 cups salad greens

1 cup shredded Prairie Breeze cheese or gruyère cheese

1 cup sliced mushrooms

½ large red onion, thinly sliced

Microgreens, for garnish (optional)

TO MAKE THE DRESSING

In a small bowl, whisk together all the ingredients and set aside.

TO MAKE THE SALAD

In a large sauté pan over medium heat, cook the bacon to desired level of doneness. Transfer the bacon to a plate lined with paper towels, leaving the drippings in the pan.

Keep the pan over medium heat. You only need about 2 tablespoons of bacon drippings; if you have too much, just spoon some out and set aside for another use. Add the potatoes and season with the pepper. Cook until the potatoes are crisp on the outside but fork-tender. Transfer the potatoes to a plate and top with tented aluminum foil to keep them warm.

Break the bacon into large pieces (approximately ½ inch long).

Wipe out the pan used to fry the potatoes, or heat a second pan over medium heat. Add the butter. Crack the eggs into the pan and season with the salt and pepper and cook to desired doneness. To make them sunny-side up, cover the pan and cook for about 3 or 4 minutes, until the whites are set but the yolks are still runny. Remove from the heat.

In a large bowl, toss the greens with the dressing, then divide evenly onto 4 plates. Sprinkle each plate with the cheese, mushrooms, onion, fried potatoes, and bacon. Top each plate with 1 egg. Garnish with microgreens, if using, and serve.

WHERE TO FIND...

Greens, Potatoes	Prairie Breeze Cheese	Bacon
Cleverley Farms	Milton Creamery	Niman Ranch
Mingo, IA	Milton, IA	IA

Maggie Pleskac

CHEF MAGGIE'S VEGETARIAN CAFÉ | 311 N. 8TH ST. | LINCOLN, NE |
402.477.3959 | MAGGIESVEGETARIAN.COM

The rain is soft and continuous outside Maggie Pleskac's home. It is June, and the season has arrived unexpectedly early. She's already harvested mature garlic from her garden, which she uses to supply food for both her family and her restaurant, Maggie's Vegetarian Café in Lincoln.

Inside, she sits in the lotus position on a living room chair. She is in excellent shape, due to her near-religious commitment to yoga and her strict organic and vegetable-heavy eating habits.

Her home is decorated with bright colors, just like the café she opened in 2000. Her goal remains the same today as it was then: to positively impact her community, one bite at a time. At that time, 25-year-old Maggie had a love of all things California and was strongly influenced by the fresh, local food culture she had experienced while living there in her early 20s. Embracing a similar concept for her tiny 500-square-foot café seemed logical, even in "The Beef State." Nearly a decade before farm to table was trendy in Nebraska, Maggie hung photos of her farm partners on her restaurant walls. In the years since she opened, her order-at-the-window café she has built a strong and loyal following.

"If one thrives, we all thrive. It's a community-based model. If I buy my bread from John, then he is going to buy a sandwich from me. If he buys a sandwich from me, then he is supporting Harvest Home, whose tomatoes I used," Maggie says.

Community-supported agriculture (CSA) programs, where consumers prepay for weekly deliveries of farm-fresh produce, are becoming more commonplace in private homes, but what Maggie would really like to see is something she refers to as "RSA," or restaurant-supported agriculture. Getting a surprise box of vegetables each week inspires her creativity as a chef and maintains her passion for feeding people healthy vegetarian meals. Opening her café was not only about her lifestyle choices but also about embracing the opportunity to support others who seek healthy, local, meat-free options.

"I truly believe that if you build something that does the most good for the most people, it cannot fail."

"I truly believe that if you build something that does the most good for the most people, it cannot fail," Maggie says, pausing for a minute to think. "[I knew] if I could create many forks and many plates then that would make a difference."

For Maggie, being a good steward means feeding her family and customers food that fosters a healthy environment and supports farmers who likely harvested the ingredients for the meal she served just before it rained on a warm June day. ■

Roasted Rhubarb and Asparagus Pasta Salad

SERVES 4–6

Rhubarb is most often used in desserts, sweetened with sugar. Here, the rhubarb is savory, with a bright, citrus-like appeal complemented by lemony sorrel, which can be difficult to find but grows easily in a home garden. This dish is equally delicious hot or cold, which makes it adaptable to Nebraska's unpredictable spring weather. If you can't find sorrel, feel free to substitute with any fresh herb.

Rhubarb can be red or green, and thick or thin. You want the pieces in this dish to hold together, so adjust the roasting time based on the thickness of your rhubarb.

—Maggie Pleskac MAGGIE'S VEGETARIAN CAFÉ | LINCOLN, NE

½ pound bowtie pasta

¼ pound spinach leaves, coarsely chopped, thicker stems removed

½ pound rhubarb (about 2 large stalks), cut into ½-inch pieces

½ pound asparagus stalks, cut into 1-inch pieces

2 tablespoons olive oil, plus more to taste

2 large cloves garlic, chopped

½ teaspoon sea salt, plus more to taste and for the pasta water

½ teaspoon red pepper flakes, plus more to taste

1 small handful fresh basil leaves, thinly sliced (about 2 tablespoons)

1 small handful fresh sorrel leaves, thinly sliced (about 2 tablespoons) (optional)

Preheat the oven to 375°F.

Bring a large pot of salted water to a boil, and begin to cook the pasta according to the package instructions.

Meanwhile, place the spinach in the bottom of a colander and set aside.

In a large bowl, toss the rhubarb and asparagus with the olive oil, garlic, salt, and red pepper flakes. Spread the mixture evenly onto a baking sheet and roast for 6 to 8 minutes, or until just fork-tender. You don't want the rhubarb to break apart.

When the pasta has finished cooking, pour it into the colander with the chopped spinach. The hot water will wilt the spinach. Drain the spinach and pasta, and transfer to a large serving dish. Add the rhubarb mixture, basil, and sorrel, if using. Toss together, then add more olive oil, salt, and pepper to taste. Serve.

WHERE TO FIND...

Rhubarb	Spinach	Basil	Garlic
Common Good Farm	Shadow Brook Farm	Harvest Home Waverly, NE	Community CROPS
Raymond, NE	Lincoln, NE		Lincoln, NE

Blue Broccoli Soup

SERVES 6–8

This versatile recipe can be used to make a creamy soup out of whatever vegetable is plentiful at the time. Our favorite is broccoli. You may want to adjust the type of cheese based on the veggies you have. An immersion blender pulls this soup together quickly.

—Charlotte and John Hamburger BACK ALLEY BAKERY | HASTINGS, NE

4 tablespoons butter

1 medium onion, diced

4 stalks celery, diced

2 large russet potatoes, peeled and cubed

4 cups chicken stock, vegetable stock, or water

1 fresh bay leaf

1–2 cups broccoli florets, broken into spoon-sized pieces

3 cups chopped broccoli stems (peeled if woody)

½ teaspoon ground nutmeg

½ teaspoon dried basil

2 cups half-and-half

1½ cups crumbled blue cheese

Salt and freshly ground black pepper, to taste

WHERE TO FIND...

Broccoli
26th Street Farm
Hastings, NE

In a large pot over medium heat, melt the butter. Add the onion and celery and sauté until soft. Add the potatoes, stock, and bay leaf and bring to a boil. Reduce to a simmer and continue to cook until the potatoes are tender, about 15 minutes.

Meanwhile, in a small pot, steam the broccoli florets, then set aside.

Add the broccoli stems, nutmeg, and basil to the pot with the potatoes and stock. Simmer for about 5 minutes. Turn off the heat; remove and discard the bay leaf. Using an immersion blender, purée the mixture; you can also use a blender to purée in batches. Stir in the steamed florets, half-and-half, and blue cheese. Gently heat to warm through. Season to taste with the salt and pepper. Ladle into bowls and serve.

Spring Garlic Soup

SERVES 6

Spring garlic, also known as green garlic, has a mild, soft flavor. It, along with garlic scapes (the curled necks that emerge from the bulb), is one of the first gifts of the season. It is harvested between April and June, before the garlic paper surrounds each clove, which means there is no need to peel it. Simply cut off the root end and remove the fibrous stem, then prepare this delicate soup.

—*Jason Simon* ALBA | DES MOINES, IA

½ pound spring garlic, chopped into 2-inch pieces

2 Yukon gold potatoes, sliced into 1-inch chips

1 medium yellow onion, peeled and quartered

3 radishes, halved

1 carrot, peeled and sliced into 1-inch pieces

½ cup water

1 tablespoon olive oil, plus more for garnish

4 cups whole milk

4 cups chicken stock

2 fresh bay leaves

Pinch ground saffron

Salt and freshly ground black pepper, to taste

Saffron threads, for garnish

WHERE TO FIND…

Spring Garlic
Cleverley Farms
Mingo, IA

Preheat the oven to 400°F.

In a large roasting pan or Dutch oven, place the garlic, potatoes, onion, radishes, carrot, water, and olive oil. Cover with aluminum foil or a lid and roast for 25 minutes.

Meanwhile, in a large stockpot, combine the milk, stock, bay leaves, and saffron and bring to a simmer.

Once the vegetables are done roasting, remove the bay leaves from the milk mixture and discard.

In a blender, combine the vegetables in batches with 1 or 2 cups of the milk mixture. Purée until smooth, then transfer to a large bowl. Repeat the process until all of the vegetables are puréed and silky. To keep yourself from getting burned, do not overfill the blender with hot liquid.

Once the soup is completely puréed, season to taste with the salt and pepper. Transfer the soup to individual bowls and garnish each with a few saffron threads and dots of olive oil before serving.

Bryce Coulton

CHEF THE FRENCH BULLDOG | 5003 UNDERWOOD AVE. | OMAHA, NE |
402.505.4633 | FRENCHBULLDOGOMAHA.COM

Bryce Coulton's voice has a slow New Jersey swagger. He speaks deliberately and with precision, much in the same way he maneuvers a curved boning knife across the hindquarter of a butchered pig. The morning of our interview, I watch as he practices charcuterie, the craft of preserving meat, in his restaurant's back kitchen.

"This piece," he says while pausing briefly, gently pressing his fingertips into the raw flesh, "will be used to make Calabrian salami."

Bryce might be the perfect person to recreate the generations-old salami from southern Italy. He lived there for 5 years, during his 20-plus years in the military, which then landed him in Omaha—but not before exposing him to the foods and flavors of Italy, England, and, most importantly, Ireland, where he learned his trade at the Ballymaloe Cookery School. While at Ballymaloe (a school whose founder, Darina Allen, is to Ireland what Alice Waters is to the United States), Bryce found butchering to be one of the more interesting aspects of his culinary education, and charcuterie to be the most challenging. Creating salumi that taste as beautiful as they sound—soppressata, finocchiona, bresaola, and mortadella—requires a combination of cuts of meat, fats, salts, spices, bacteria, temperature, and time.

"One day, we brought in a pig and spent 10 hours processing it from head to toe. We learned about every single aspect of it, but most importantly we learned how to appreciate it and make the best use of the animal, which is something I wanted to carry on," explains Bryce.

Like many things in the food world, what was old is new again. Though charcuterie was originally developed as a preservation method, it is now primarily practiced for the flavors it creates. Following old-world traditions, Bryce believes in knowing his farmers, noting that proximity to producers is paramount.

"Much of the product I deal with is literally down the road, which gives me a great opportunity to build relationships with these farmers," he says. "I've even eaten raw pork. I don't know if that proves my stupidity, or my trust . . ." ■

Creating salumi that taste as beautiful as they sound—soppressata, finocchiona, bresaola, and mortadella—requires a combination of cuts of meat, fats, salts, spices, bacteria, temperature, and time.

Country Pâté with Piccalilli

SERVES 10

A well-made country pâté is a simple and wonderful light meal. It keeps well in the fridge, about 10 days, making it available to share with friends at the drop of a hat. Once finished, cut a few slices and spoon out a few pickled vegetables, as the acidity cuts the richness of the pâté. The spices should be subtle, with the emphasis on the unique flavors of the pork. The pâté requires 1½ hours in the oven and a day to rest in the refrigerator; the vegetables for the piccalilli require 24 hours in the refrigerator, so plan accordingly.

—*Bryce Coulton* THE FRENCH BULLDOG | OMAHA, NE

PICCALILLI

1 head cauliflower, florets and stems diced into ½-inch pieces

1 cucumber, peeled, seeded, and diced into ½-inch pieces

1 onion, finely chopped

2 tablespoons kosher salt

1 cup cider vinegar

½ cup granulated sugar

1 tablespoon ground turmeric

1 tablespoon mustard seeds

1 tablespoon red pepper flakes

1 tablespoon finely chopped fresh ginger

½ teaspoon ground nutmeg

½ teaspoon ground cayenne pepper

1 tablespoon Dijon mustard

1 tablespoon all-purpose flour

COUNTRY PÂTÉ

1 cup heavy cream

¼ cup fresh breadcrumbs

1½ pounds lean pork, ground

4 teaspoons kosher salt

1 star anise, ground

½ teaspoon freshly ground black pepper

½ teaspoon ground allspice

¼ teaspoon ground white pepper

¼ teaspoon ground nutmeg

¼ teaspoon ground ginger

½ pound pork liver, cut into 1-inch cubes

½ pound fatback, ground

2 eggs

Crusty bread or crackers, for serving

WHERE TO FIND...

Cucumber, Cauliflower, Onion
Rhizosphere Farm
Missouri Valley, IA

Pork
Truebridge Foods
Omaha, NE

TO MAKE THE PICCALILLI

In a large bowl, coat the cauliflower, cucumber, and onion with the salt and toss to combine. Transfer to a strainer set over the large bowl and let drain overnight in the refrigerator. The following day, rinse the vegetables, drain, and set aside.

In a large pot, combine the vinegar, sugar, spices, and Dijon mustard. Warm over low heat, until the sugar dissolves. Add the vegetables to the pot and bring to a boil, then reduce to a simmer. Cook for 20 to 30 minutes, until the vegetables are just softened. Sprinkle in the flour and stir gently to thicken the liquid. Let cool, then store in the refrigerator. The piccalilli will keep for 3 weeks.

TO MAKE THE PÂTÉ

Preheat the oven to 275°F.

Grease a loaf pan (8 or 10 inch is fine) or a 1½-quart terrine mold, then line it with parchment paper, extending the paper 2 inches over each end.

In a medium bowl, mix together the heavy cream and breadcrumbs. Place in the refrigerator. (It's important to keep the heavy cream mixture, ground pork, and fatback very cold so they don't separate when mixing.)

In a large bowl, combine the lean pork and all of the spices. Mix with your hands until evenly distributed. Transfer to a food processor and mix for 1 minute. Add the liver and continue to mix for 1 more minute. Add the fatback, mixing for 1 minute, until the fat is well combined. Next, add the eggs and mix for 30 seconds.

Remove the cream mixture from the refrigerator, give it a quick stir, and add it to the food processor, mixing for 1 minute. The pâté will look shiny and smooth, with bits of liver about the size of oats.

Pour the mixture into the prepared pan, folding the parchment over the top of the exposed mixture. Cover the pan with aluminum foil and place into a 9 × 13-inch baking pan. Fill the baking pan with water so that the water level reaches ⅔ of the way up the loaf pan. This cooking method, which is called a bain-marie, allows the pâté to cook evenly by distributing the heat throughout the water. Bake for approximately 1½ hours, or until the pâté's internal temperature reaches 140°F on an instant-read thermometer. Remove from the bain-marie and let cool. The pâté will continue to cook once removed from the oven, ultimately bringing the temperature to 145°F.

Place in the refrigerator overnight. The following day, remove the pâté from the loaf pan, scrape away any fat, wrap the pâté with plastic wrap, and store in the refrigerator until ready to serve. Cut into ½-inch-thick slices and serve with the piccalilli and crusty bread or crackers.

Nick Strawhecker

CHEF DANTE RISTORANTE PIZZERIA | 16901 WRIGHT PLAZA | OMAHA, NE |
402.932.3078 | WWW.DANTEPIZZERIA.COM

Nick Strawhecker is matter of fact about food and the journey that brought him to it. He always knew he wanted a restaurant, and that local food would play a dominant role in it—not because it was trendy, or even to reduce his carbon footprint, but quite simply because he likes food and thinks it should taste good.

Anyone who has ever sampled a store-bought tomato in the middle of February understands that it's just a mealy stand-in for the sweet and acidic orbs that are sun-ripened on a hot August day. Seasonal ingredients harvested at the height of perfection are a chef's dream. They enable talented craftsmen like Nick to transform earthy Italian dishes from mere sustenance to swoon worthy.

Rhizosphere Farm in Missouri Valley, Iowa, supplies much of the produce used at Dante Ristorante Pizzeria, while Branched Oak Farm in Raymond, Nebraska, supplies between 160 and 300 pounds of creamy, freshly made mozzarella per week, from its small dairy herd. For Nick, anticipating the best of every season from producers is as invigorating as using their products to create new menu components daily.

"It's just so obvious why I would have a place like this and use local products. It's better for you and it tastes better—what is there not to get?"

"Krista Dittman from Branched Oak is our biggest food source," explains Nick. "She is great. She is honest. She cares as much as I do. She loves our place. We love her product. And we both have the same views on food—staying local, eating whole. To me, it's just so obvious why I would have a place like this and use local products. It's better for you and it tastes better—what is there not to get?"

Born in Omaha, Nick spent his teen years living in and traveling throughout Europe at a time when kids wouldn't think to ask for chicken nuggets.

"You ate what adults ate. I remember traveling to Brussels for the weekend and my Dad and I would dig into bowls of mussels. There

wasn't anything weird about it; I just loved it," he says.

Although wood-fired pizza is an important component of his offerings, a deep respect for the farm-to-table interpretation of rustic Italian dishes has been critical to the restaurant's success. It's also a nod to Nick's time spent in Italy, where he experienced hyper-local cuisine and food served not only to nourish but also to represent the environment and reflect the culture.

"We didn't even eat from the region in some of those places—it was the town," says Nick, who feels fortunate to be part of Omaha's cultural food revolution. His enthusiasm over spicy and bitter greens during the hot summer months and freshly pulled mozzarella from grass-fed cows translates into delicious and local food experiences for all who enter Dante. Perhaps, eating solely from the town isn't too far off. ■

Braised Chicken Soup with Potato Gnocchi and Morel Mushrooms

SERVES 8

This dish is a perfect Sunday dinner for a cool spring day. It's light but cozy, and the ultimate comfort food. Start the day before you want to eat, as the chicken needs 24 hours to brine. The recipe requires about four hours of hands-on time, but that can be cut in half if you make the gnocchi ahead of time and freeze them. If you don't want to break down a whole chicken, you can always ask your processor or butcher to do this for you, which saves even more time.

—*Nick Strawhecker* DANTE RISTORANTE PIZZERIA | OMAHA, NE

CHICKEN AND BRINE

1 whole chicken

2 cups water

¼ cup salt

¼ cup granulated sugar

3 sprigs fresh thyme

3 sprigs fresh rosemary

3 cloves garlic, crushed

3 tablespoons black peppercorns

2 fresh bay leaves

1 lemon, halved

1 pound ice

GNOCCHI

⅓ cup plus ½ teaspoon salt, divided

7 large russet potatoes

3 tablespoons finely shredded Grana Padano cheese

½ cup all-purpose flour, plus more for dusting

Freshly ground black pepper, to taste

2 egg yolks

1 egg

2 teaspoons olive oil

SOUP

3 tablespoons olive oil, divided

1 tablespoon butter

3⅔ cups diced carrots, divided

⅔ cup diced celery

⅔ cup diced onion

2 cups cremini mushrooms

4 cloves garlic, crushed

4 sprigs fresh thyme

1 cup dry white wine

12 cups chicken stock

2 cups morel mushrooms

Salt and freshly ground black pepper, to taste

1 tablespoon minced chives

WHERE TO FIND...

Chicken
Plum Creek Farms
Burchard, NE

Carrots, Herbs, Potatoes
Rhizosphere Farm
Missouri Valley, IA

TO BRINE THE CHICKEN

Cut up the chicken, leaving everything on the bone. Cover and place in the refrigerator.

In a large pot, combine all the other brine ingredients except for the ice. Bring to a boil.

Meanwhile, place a strainer over a bowl large enough to hold the liquid, chicken, and ice. After the brine comes to a boil, pour it through the strainer into the bowl. Remove and discard the solids left in the strainer.

Add the ice to the bowl of brine. Once completely cool, add the chicken pieces. Cover and chill in the refrigerator overnight.

Continued

TO START THE GNOCCHI AND THE SOUP

Preheat the oven to 375°F.

Pour ⅓ cup of the salt onto a baking sheet. Prick the potatoes a couple of times with a fork, place on top of the salt, and roast in the oven for about 1½ hours, until the potatoes are soft.

Prepare the soup ingredients while the potatoes roast. The gnocchi will need to come together quickly once the potatoes have finished cooking. Take the chicken pieces from the refrigerator, remove them from the brine, and pat them dry with a paper towel. Discard the brine.

In a large Dutch oven, heat 2 tablespoons of the oil over medium–high heat. When it begins to shimmer, add the butter. Be careful, as it could splatter. Once the butter is melted, add the chicken, skin side down. It's important not to overcrowd the pan. Do this in batches so you get a decent sear. When the skin has developed a deep color and you have some brown bits in the bottom of the Dutch oven, remove the chicken and set aside.

If you want less fat, you can spoon some out now; just make sure you leave at least 3 tablespoons' worth in the Dutch oven. Add ⅔ cup of the diced carrots, the celery, and the onion to the Dutch oven. Stir occasionally. When the vegetables have taken on a little color, add the cremini mushrooms and sauté for about 3 minutes. Add the garlic and thyme and sauté for another minute. Add the wine and scrape the bottom of the pan to pick up the little brown bits. Add the stock and bring to a boil. Remove from the heat.

Remove and discard the skin from the chicken breast only, then add all the chicken into the Dutch oven. Cover tightly with aluminum foil and then put the lid on. When the potatoes are finished, remove them from the oven and then place the Dutch oven into the oven. Bake for 2½ hours.

TO MAKE THE GNOCCHI

Make sure you have a clean, smooth countertop to work on. Halve the potatoes and scoop out the flesh while still warm. Push the potato flesh through a potato ricer directly onto the countertop. You can also mash them in a bowl; just make sure you don't overwork the dough, as that will make the gnocchi dense rather than light and fluffy.

Once you've finished ricing the potatoes, sprinkle the cheese evenly on top and add the flour, the remaining ½ teaspoon of the salt, and about 5 twists of the pepper grinder. Form a long, shallow well in the potatoes; pour in the egg yolks, egg, and olive oil. Using a bench scraper or stiff spatula, cut the ingredients together until they have formed a loose dough. Knead the dough for about 2 minutes, dusting with a little flour if it's too sticky.

Pull off segments of the dough and roll into cylinders about the thickness of your thumb. Cut into sections about 1 inch long. The gnocchi should be soft and tender and resemble little pillows. Place them on a lightly floured baking sheet and cover with plastic wrap.

Bring a large pot of water to a simmer, not a boil, and add the gnocchi in batches. They should take only about 45 seconds to 1 minute to cook, and will float when ready. Scoop them out with a slotted spoon, place them onto a plate, and set aside.

TO ASSEMBLE THE DISH

When the chicken is done, remove it from the Dutch oven, reserving the cooking liquid. Pull the meat from the bones, making sure to check for small bones. Discard the skin and bones. Strain the reserved liquid and discard the solids. This liquid is your soup base.

Wipe out the Dutch oven and place it on the stovetop over medium–high heat. Add the remaining 1 tablespoon of the olive oil. Once the oil shimmers, add the remaining 3 cups of the carrots. Once the carrots have a little color, add the reserved soup base. Scrape the bottom of the pan to pick up any brown bits, then add the pulled chicken and morel mushrooms. Season to taste with the salt and pepper. Stir in the cooked gnocchi just so they warm through. Spoon into wide, shallow bowls. Top with the chives and serve.

Note: You can make the gnocchi days, weeks, or even months ahead of time and freeze. Place them on a baking sheet lined with parchment paper and put the baking sheet in the freezer. Once frozen, transfer the gnocchi into a plastic bag. The cooking time is still about 1 minute.

Lavender-Crusted Rack of Lamb with Asparagus, Morel Ragù, and Potato Purée

SERVES 4

Prepare all of the ingredients for each step ahead of time, as the dish will come together quickly once you get started. You can even blanch the asparagus the day before to save some time and stove space.

   This recipe calls for the rack of lamb to be frenched (which means the meat, fat, and membranes that connect the ribs are removed, leaving part of the rib bones exposed). If you don't want to french the lamb yourself, ask your butcher or processor to do this for you when you order.

   If dried lavender is unavailable, you can omit it; the rub is still delicious without it.

—*Benjamin Smart* BIG GROVE BREWERY | SOLON, IA

ASPARAGUS

16 stalks asparagus, thick
   bottoms removed

4 tablespoons unsalted butter

2 tablespoons minced shallots

Juice of ½ lemon

Salt, to taste

POTATO PURÉE

8 large Yukon gold potatoes,
   peeled and diced large

2 sticks unsalted butter, cubed

1 cup heavy cream

Salt and ground white pepper,
   to taste

RACK OF LAMB

1 rack of lamb, frenched

30 allspice berries

3 cloves garlic

2 tablespoons dried lavender

1 tablespoon coriander seeds

1 stick cinnamon

1 teaspoon black peppercorns

1 teaspoon cumin seeds

Zest of 1 lemon

Salt

12 fresh bay leaves

6 sprigs fresh thyme

Thinly sliced fresh mint, for garnish

MOREL RAGÙ

4 cups morel mushrooms

2 large shallots, minced

2 cloves garlic, minced

1 cup chicken stock

3 teaspoons sherry vinegar

4 tablespoons unsalted butter

Salt and freshly ground black
   pepper, to taste

2 tablespoons thinly sliced chives

WHERE TO FIND...

Lamb
Pavelka's Point Meats
Mount Vernon, IA

Asparagus
Kroul Farms
Mount Vernon, IA

TO MAKE THE ASPARAGUS

Preheat the oven to 325°F.

Bring a large, heavily salted pot of water to boil. Set a bowl of ice water nearby. Add the asparagus stalks to the boiling water for about 60 seconds to blanch. Immediately plunge the stalks in the ice water for 60 seconds to stop the cooking process. Transfer to a plate lined with paper towels and set aside.

In a medium sauté pan over medium–high heat, melt the butter. Add the shallots and sweat for about 1 minute. Add the blanched asparagus, increase the heat to high, and sauté until the asparagus is slightly blistered and heated

Continued

through. The asparagus should still have a pleasant bite to it and not be mushy at all. Remove from the heat, dress with the lemon juice, and season to taste with the salt, if desired. Transfer the asparagus and shallots to a plate and wipe out the pan for later use.

TO MAKE THE POTATO PURÉE AND THE LAMB

In a large pot of water, bring the potatoes to barely a simmer.

Meanwhile, divide the rack of lamb so you have 2 sections with 4 bones each.

To make the spice rub, combine the allspice berries through the lemon zest in a spice mill and grind. Sprinkle the rub over a baking sheet.

Salt the lamb. Dredge the front and back of the lamb in the rub. Allow it to sit for 10 minutes for the spices to fully adhere. This prevents the rub from falling off the meat when you sear it.

Heat a grill or large cast-iron pan over medium–high heat. Set a roasting rack or cooling rack over a baking sheet. Sear the lamb on both sides. Transfer to the prepared rack. Wrap the frenched bones in aluminum foil, but leave the meat exposed. Top the lamb with the bay leaves and thyme sprigs. Roast in the oven until the internal temperature of the lamb reaches 130°F to 135°F, about 10 minutes. The lamb should be medium-rare to medium.

While the lamb is in the oven, finish up the potatoes and get started on the mushroom ragù.

The potatoes are ready when the tip of a knife pierces them without any resistance. Once they are cooked, drain and pass them through a potato ricer or food mill. You could also use a potato masher. Add the cubed butter and stir with a spoon until the butter is fully incorporated. Add the cream and stir until the potatoes are a silky consistency and not too stiff. Season to taste with the salt and white pepper. Keep warm over low heat.

Remove the lamb from the oven, tent with aluminum foil, and let it rest for 15 minutes.

TO MAKE THE MOREL RAGÙ AND ASSEMBLE THE DISH

Rinse the morel mushrooms in warm water, gently agitating them to remove any debris. Dry them on paper towels.

In the dry sauté pan (the one you used for the asparagus), sauté the mushrooms over medium–high heat. The mushrooms will begin to release their moisture; once most of that moisture is evaporated, about 1 to 2 minutes, add the minced shallots and garlic. Cook for an additional minute. Add the chicken stock and let it reduce by half. Add the sherry vinegar and remove from the heat. Swirl in the butter to emulsify. Season to taste with the salt and pepper, and fold in the chives. Add the asparagus stalks to the pan just to warm them up.

To serve, remove the aluminum foil and herbs from the rack of lamb. Cut the lamb, following the bone down through the meat, leaving 1 bone per slice of rack. You should have 8 individual pieces of lamb when you're finished. Put a large spoonful of potato purée on each plate. Spoon a generous amount of morel ragù on top. Place 4 stalks of asparagus on top of the ragù. Place 2 pieces of lamb over the asparagus. Scatter the fresh mint about the plate and serve.

Sunchoke Gnocchi with Rosa Maria and Peas

SERVES 4

These little lumps are a good measure of the attention to detail that goes into even simple preparations. Good gnocchi are lighter than air. Overwork the dough and the gnocchi become chewy and dense; underwork it and the gnocchi fall apart.
    Rosa Maria is a creamy, semihard goat cheese that adds the perfect finish to the dish.

—*Paul Kulik* THE BOILER ROOM | OMAHA, NE

1 pound russet potatoes
    (about 3 large)

⅓ pound sunchokes, peeled

1 egg

1 teaspoon sea salt, divided

¼ teaspoon ground nutmeg

¼ teaspoon ground cayenne
    pepper

½ cup all-purpose flour, plus
    more for dusting

Olive oil, for coating

4 tablespoons butter

3 cloves garlic, crushed

¼ teaspoon red pepper flakes

2 tablespoons grated Rosa Maria
    cheese, plus more shaved,
    for garnish

4 teaspoons fresh lemon juice

¼ cup peas, blanched

4 sugar snap peapods, thinly
    sliced on the bias

Pea tendrils, for garnish (optional)

WHERE TO FIND...

Rosa Maria
Dutch Girl Creamery
Lincoln, NE

Potatoes
Blooms Organic
Crescent, IA

Peas
Squeaky Green Organics
Omaha, NE

Preheat the oven to 375°F.

Wrap the unpeeled potatoes and the peeled sunchokes individually in aluminum foil and bake until tender, about 45 minutes to 1 hour.

In a small bowl, whisk together the egg, ¾ teaspoon of the salt, the nutmeg, and the cayenne pepper until thoroughly incorporated and somewhat frothy.

Once the potatoes and sunchokes are tender, halve the potatoes and scoop out the flesh while they're still warm. Push the potato flesh and the sunchokes through a potato ricer and into a medium bowl. Using a large spoon or firm spatula, cut in the egg mixture. Carefully cut in the flour. Fold the dough a few times until it forms a ball. Do not overwork it, or your gnocchi will be too dense. The dough will be sticky.

Dust your hands and the work surface with flour. Pinch off some dough and roll it into long logs as thick as your thumb. Cut the log into little pieces about 1 inch long. Press each piece gently onto the tines of the back of a fork, then roll it over so it forms a little pillow with tine impressions on it.

When finished making gnocchi out of all of the dough, bring a large pot of salted water to a boil and drop in the gnocchi. Cook until they float, about 1 minute. Remove the gnocchi from the water with a slotted spoon, place on a plate, and coat with the olive oil. Save the water.

In a large sauté pan, melt the butter. Add the crushed garlic, the remaining ¼ teaspoon of the salt, and the red pepper flakes. When the butter smells nutty and begins to brown, add the gnocchi. This should take a few minutes. Add the grated Rosa Maria. Add the lemon juice and 1 teaspoon of the gnocchi water. Add the blanched peas. Cook just until warmed through. Divide into 4 portions. Top with the sliced peapods. Garnish with the shaved Rosa Maria and the pea tendrils, if using, and serve.

Note: Sunchokes, also known as Jerusalem artichokes, look a bit like fresh ginger root. To peel the sunchokes, break off any large protrusions to remove any dirt caught in the crevasses, then use a paring knife to gently scrape away the skin.

Clayton Chapman

CHEF THE GREY PLUME | 220 S. 31ST AVE., SUITE 3101 | OMAHA, NE |
402.763.4447 | WWW.THEGREYPLUME.COM

On any given morning, passersby might catch a peek of a platinum-blond boy stirring raw coffee beans on a prep countertop or walking between the white linen-covered tables wearing puppy pajamas and rocking a pair of black cowboy boots.

When I visited, a little red, blue, and yellow push car sat near the entrance to the kitchen, awaiting its rider: Hudson Grey. The sleepy boy was passed gently to Clayton Chapman, while Hudson's mom, Bernadette, started peeling off layers, first a stocking cap and then a blue-and-green sweater. Clayton stood holding his two-year-old son, pretended to gobble up his hands, then disappeared with him into the kitchen, his voice trailing behind him, "Are you ready for breakfast?"

Moments later, Bernadette sat down at the amber-hued chef's table to tell me about what life is like as a restaurant family. Clayton brought her freshly roasted coffee in a french press, served on a silver platter as if she were any other diner at The Grey Plume. Hudson came running out of the kitchen to greet the toy that had been patiently waiting for him.

It is this gentle sense of ease and family togetherness that permeates The Grey Plume. It might also be why diners are certain to feel this "come as you are" comfort while eating some of the most technically difficult and tastefully composed contemporary cuisine in the region. Sure, the seasonally driven restaurant earned national recognition the first week it opened for being the greenest restaurant in America, but being green is really a sidebar to the deeper story: how a love of food and family brought them to this place; a group of people who are confident of their purpose in life and on the brink of imminent success.

> *"This whole thing, it's more of a calling than anything."*

"I think it's the right thing to do—this whole thing, it's more of a calling than anything," Clayton said later that morning. "I mean, I've been in the restaurant industry since I was 13. I've known since I started that I was never getting out of it."

Throughout the morning one thing was noticeably absent—a giant refrigeration truck. Instead, one by one, a farmer, a producer, and a rancher walked in wheeling a cooler and exchanged pleasantries or sometimes just a wave before delivering what was sure to be part of that evening's meal.

"Food in its most primary form is nourishment," Clayton said briefly, then paused, putting his chin on his hand and looking out the window toward Farnam Street. The day was sunny and beams of light filtered through the ivory curtains. Clayton has a very serious, no-bones-about-it approach to things. Not to say he doesn't enjoy a good joke, but his outlook is of the old-world sense that hard work and a humble nature is the only way to get what you want out of life. "It's more than that to me; it's a way of life to me—it is life. It's what our life revolves around—that life cycle of food, planning, setting the list, picking seeds, working with the growers. Then you wait and you wait and you wait for the bounty; then you have the height of the harvest where everything is in its freshest form."

The everyday diner can easily search a restaurant website to find it boasting about how it uses locally sourced food. Few establishments, however, can match Clayton's ability to share how the bison served for dinner that night was raised, the time it takes to churn butter, or even the educational process required on both sides of the table to bring food from the farm to the fork.

Everything—tomato marmalade, antique clocks, canned peaches, a chef's table—has a story, which is why eating at The Grey Plume feels like a dinner party at your best friend's house. Places with soul are filled with things that have meaning. If food can be considered the heartbeat of a family, then The Grey Plume is the pulse of its community, using culinary expertise and gentle pressure to reshape the concept, the flavor, and the experience of local food. ■

RECIPES FROM CLAYTON:

Lamb on a Bed of Sautéed Spring Vegetables

SERVES 4

The first thing I think of when spring comes around is lamb and lighter vegetables. Dakota Harvest Farm lamb is certified grass fed and certified humane, and produced by Bob Corio.

A ramp is a wild spring onion that grows near water in damp forest areas. It is my absolute favorite ingredient to work with. If you can find a local forager for ramps, hold onto him or her for dear life! If you can't find ramps, feel free to use scallions. It's best to prepare all the vegetables before starting this recipe, as it comes together quickly.

—Clayton Chapman THE GREY PLUME | OMAHA, NE

LAMB

2 racks of lamb

Kosher salt and freshly ground black pepper, to taste

2 tablespoons vegetable oil

3 sprigs fresh rosemary, divided

4 tablespoons unsalted butter

VEGETABLES

1 tablespoon vegetable oil

16 ramps (leaves separated from the bulbs)

10 breakfast radishes, quartered

2 cloves garlic (skin on)

5 tablespoons unsalted butter

1½ cups spring peas, blanched

2 tablespoons George Paul red wine vinegar

Salt and freshly ground black pepper, to taste

Minced chives, for garnish

WHERE TO FIND...

Lamb	Breakfast
Dakota Harvest Farm	Radishes
Jefferson, SD	Blooms Organic
	Crescent, IA
Peas	
Honey Creek Farms	Vinegar
Oakland, IA	George Paul Vinegar
	Cody, NE

TO MAKE THE LAMB

Preheat the oven to 350°F.

Trim the fat and silver skin from the lamb. Working with 1 rack at a time, divide each into 4 chops with 2 bones each. Season each chop generously with the kosher salt and pepper.

Heat a large sauté pan over medium-high heat, then add the oil. Add 1 sprig of the rosemary to the pan, then sear the lamb chops on all sides until golden brown. (You may have to do this in stages based on the size of your pan.) Searing should take about 2 minutes per side. Once the meat has a nice crust, place it on a baking sheet. Melt the butter and then brush it all over the lamb chops. Keep the pan for the vegetables.

Cut the remaining rosemary into shorter sprigs, then top each chop with some. Place the chops in the oven and roast until the internal temperature reaches about 138°F. This should only take 10 to 15 minutes. You want the final temperature to be about 140°F to 142°F degrees before you eat. (Removing the lamb from the oven at 138° allows the meat to rest, and it will continue cooking to reach the desired temperature.) Once cooked, keep warm until ready to serve.

TO MAKE THE VEGETABLES

Using the same pan in which you seared the lamb, heat the oil over medium-high heat. Once the oil is hot, add the ramp bulbs, radishes, and garlic cloves. Sauté the vegetables until they have a little bit of golden color. Add the butter and allow it to foam; this usually takes 1 minute. Add the peas and ramp leaves, followed by the vinegar. Season to taste with the salt and pepper. Garnish with the chives.

Place a bed of vegetables on each of 4 plates, and then top with a lamb chop. Serve immediately.

Beet Salad with Goat Cheese Cream and Passion Fruit Marshmallow (p. 50)

Beet Salad with Goat Cheese Cream and Passion Fruit Marshmallow

SERVES 8–10 | PICTURED ON P. 48

Admittedly, beet and marshmallow isn't a traditional pairing, but it's one of our most popular dishes at the restaurant. This is a great first plate for a dinner party. All the steps can be done ahead of time and assembled quickly just before serving.

—*Sean Wilson* PROOF | DES MOINES, IA

MARSHMALLOW

1 cup passion fruit juice, chilled

3 teaspoons gelatin

⅔ cup granulated sugar

2 tablespoons plus 1 teaspoon meringue powder

½ teaspoon vegetable oil

BEETS

24 baby beets, gold and red (skin on), trimmed and halved

1 orange (skin on), sliced

5 tablespoons olive oil, divided

Salt and freshly ground black pepper, to taste

2 shallots, minced (about 3 tablespoons)

TO MAKE THE MARSHMALLOW

In a small bowl, place the cold juice. Sprinkle the gelatin on top and let it sit for 5 minutes.

In a medium saucepan over medium heat, whisk together the juice mixture and sugar until the sugar has dissolved and the mixture comes to a simmer. Pour into the bowl of your stand mixture and let cool to room temperature. Once cool, sprinkle in the meringue power.

Place the bowl into your stand mixer fitted with the whisk attachment, and whip the mixture until semi-stiff peaks form, about 10 minutes.

Line a small or medium baking sheet, with 1-inch sides, with parchment paper. Grease the parchment with the oil. Using a spatula, scoop the marshmallow onto the parchment and spread it so the marshmallow is about 1 inch deep. Let it set at room temperature for at least 2 hours, up to 24 hours, before serving. If you are keeping it out more than 2 hours, lightly oil another piece of parchment paper and set it on top of the marshmallow. Once the marshmallow is set and it's time to cut it, oil the blade of your knife. Cut the marshmallow into strips that are about 4 inches long, 1½ inches wide, and 1 inch deep.

TO MAKE THE BEETS

Preheat the oven to 375°F.

In a large roasting pan, place the halved beets and orange slices. Drizzle with 3 tablespoons of the olive oil and season to taste with the salt and pepper. Cover with aluminum foil. Roast for about 1 hour, until the beets are fork-tender. Remove from the oven. While still warm, rub the skin off of the beets with a towel and discard. Discard the orange slices. Quarter the beets.

In a medium bowl, toss the beets with the minced shallots and the remaining 2 tablespoons of the olive oil. Set aside.

Note: Store gold and red beets separately in a covered container in the refrigerator for up to 4 days. If you make these ahead of time, do not toss the beets in the olive oil and shallots until you're ready to serve.

PICADA

2 cups cubed country
    bread, crust removed

2 cloves garlic

2 tablespoons olive oil

½ cup shelled pistachios,
    toasted

Zest of ¾ orange

½ dried ancho chile,
    stemmed, seeded, and
    soaked in hot water

Salt and freshly ground black
    pepper, to taste

GOAT CHEESE CREAM

½ cup half-and-half

½ cup goat cheese

1 tablespoon cream cheese

FOR SERVING

1 cup microgreens, bull's
    blood beet or arugula

1 tablespoon olive oil

WHERE TO FIND...

Beets
TableTop Farm
Nevada, IA

Goat Cheese
Reichert's Dairy Air
Knoxville, IA

Garlic
Grade A Gardens
Johnston, IA

TO MAKE THE PICADA

Preheat the oven to 350°F. (Or, if you are making everything at once, simply reduce the oven heat to 350°F.)

On a baking sheet, place the cubed bread and garlic cloves in a single layer and drizzle with the olive oil. Bake, tossing the cubes a couple of times, until the bread is toasted and golden and the garlic is softened, about 15 minutes. Remove from the oven and set aside to cool to room temperature.

In a food processor, pulse the pistachios, orange zest, and chile to an even but not-too-fine texture, similar to sand. Season to taste with the salt and pepper.

Transfer the pistachio mixture to a blender. Add the cooled bread and garlic cloves and blend until smooth.

Note: The picada mixture can be stored in an airtight container for up to 3 days.

TO MAKE THE GOAT CHEESE CREAM

Place all the ingredients in a blender. Blend until smooth.

TO SERVE

On each plate, place 1 marshmallow strip. Spoon some goat cheese cream in small puddles around the plate. Place about 12 beet quarters around and on the marshmallow; sprinkle with the picada. Toss the microgreens in small bowl with the olive oil and scatter around the beets.

Note: Make the goat cheese cream up to 5 days in advance. Store covered in the refrigerator. Spread any leftovers on toast with honey and sliced apples.

Strawberry Shortcake with Rhubarb Compote

MAKES 40 3-INCH CAKES (USE 2 CAKES PER PERSON)

Simplicity is what makes this dish so good. Strawberries, slightly warm rhubarb, a delicious crumbly cake, and a dollop of cream. It's a fan favorite at the restaurant and a sure sign that spring has arrived. The cakes are actually more like cookies, and you will likely have a few left over, but no one ever complained about having too many cookies.

—Michael Haskett M.B. HASKETT DELICATESSEN | SIOUX FALLS, SD

2 eggs

2½ cups heavy cream, divided

3⅓ cups all-purpose flour

1 cup plus 1 tablespoon granulated sugar, divided

⅔ cup packed light brown sugar

1 tablespoon salt

1 tablespoon baking powder

3 sticks unsalted butter, cold

¾ cup confectioners' sugar, divided

1 pound strawberries, washed and sliced

1 pound rhubarb, cut into 1-inch slices

¼ cup water

¼ cup honey

1 tablespoon vanilla extract

WHERE TO FIND...

Strawberries, Eggs
Berrybrook Organics
Marion, SD

Rhubarb
Linda's Gardens
Chester, SD

In a small bowl, mix together the eggs and ½ cup of the heavy cream with a fork. Place in the refrigerator.

In the bowl of a stand mixer fitted with the paddle attachment, combine the flour, 1 cup of the granulated sugar, the brown sugar, the salt, and the baking powder. Give it a quick stir. Slice the butter into thin planks and add to the dry ingredients. Mix on low speed to break the butter into small pieces, about the size of a pea or smaller.

Add the cold cream mixture and continue to mix on low speed until the dough just comes together. Place in the refrigerator for 15 minutes for the butter to cool down again.

Remove the dough from the refrigerator and shape into 40 rounds a little over 1 inch in diameter. Place the rounds in a cake pan (any size is fine and you can stack the rounds if necessary), cover with plastic wrap, and let rest in the refrigerator overnight. If you must bake them the same day, just put them back in the refrigerator for a couple of hours.

When ready to bake, preheat the oven to 350°F. Line 2 baking sheets with parchment paper.

In a medium bowl, place ½ cup of the confectioners' sugar. Roll the rounds in the sugar and arrange on the prepared baking sheets. Do not crowd them, as these cakes will spread.

Bake for 11 to 13 minutes, or until the cakes are golden brown on the edges. Set aside to cool.

In a large bowl, combine the strawberries and the remaining 1 tablespoon of sugar. Gently stir a couple times, then let sit for a while before serving.

Place the rhubarb slices in a medium saucepan. Add the water and honey and bring to a slow simmer over medium heat. Cook for about 10 minutes. Stir once or twice, and remove from the heat.

In the bowl of the stand mixer fitted with the whisk attachment (or using a hand mixer), whip the remaining 2 cups of the heavy cream, the remaining ¼ cup of the confectioners' sugar, and the vanilla extract to soft peaks.

Place 1 cake on a plate, spoon a little rhubarb over it, and top with a second cake. Add a dollop of whipped cream and top with sliced strawberries. Serve.

Summer

Tesa, Poached Eggs, Roasted Tomatoes, and Spicy Cornbread (p. 58)

Tesa, Poached Eggs, Roasted Tomatoes, and Spicy Cornbread

SERVES 4

Tesa is a type of Italian bacon where the pork belly is cured flat—as opposed to pancetta, which is rolled and hung to dry for several weeks. Tesa is also unsmoked, whereas American bacon is traditionally smoked. This is the first curing project I attempted, and it set me on the path of making sausage and brining, smoking, and dry-curing meats. Because tesa is cured flat, it doesn't take up too much room in the refrigerator. Once you find yourself at the end of this process, you'll be surprised that no one told you about it sooner; you also will probably no longer be content with store-bought bacon.

The herbal complexity of tesa pairs well with the spicy cornbread and the mild warmth of poached eggs. Clearly, the only way to properly serve this meal is with a hot cup of coffee, a cold glass of juice, the morning paper, and good friends all within arm's reach.

Tesa requires 10-day advance preparation. Slice any leftovers, place in plastic bags, and freeze. The cornbread could be made a day in advance to save some time. The eggs are poached in their shells, which you can do up to three days before serving.

—Bryce Coulton THE FRENCH BULLDOG | OMAHA, NE

TESA

3 pounds pork belly, obtained from a butcher

3 tablespoons kosher salt

3 tablespoons freshly ground black pepper

3 tablespoons finely chopped garlic

2 tablespoons packed brown sugar

2 tablespoons roughly chopped fresh thyme

2 tablespoons roughly chopped fresh rosemary

2 tablespoons juniper berries, coarsely ground

1 tablespoon coarsely ground allspice

3 dried bay leaves, coarsely ground

EGGS

9 eggs, room temperature

TO MAKE THE TESA

Trim the pork belly so the edges are squared off. Depending upon how fatty the pork belly is, you may want to trim some of the fat before curing it. Fat is good, but too much is, well, too much.

In a small bowl, combine all other ingredients. Rub this mixture evenly over the pork belly.

Place the pork belly in a plastic bag, removing as much air as possible before sealing. Lay the pork flat on a plate and chill in the refrigerator for 10 days. Flip and massage the pork belly every 2 days to redistribute the spices. After 10 days, remove the tesa from the plastic bag, rinse off the spices, pat it dry, and return it to the fridge, while you prepare the other components of this meal.

TO POACH THE EGGS

Fill a large saucepan with warm water. Heat until the water reaches 145°F and maintain this temperature. (A variation of a few degrees either way is not a major concern.) Gently place the eggs, shell and all, in the water. Set a timer for 45 minutes.

When the timer sounds, remove 1 egg and gently crack it open on a small plate. The white should be cooked, but only just enough for it to hold together. A little of the outer white might slip off; that's OK. If the white of the test egg isn't fully cooked, continue to cook the remaining eggs an additional 5 minutes. If the test egg is cooked, remove the remaining eggs from the pan and place them, still intact, in a bowl of ice water. This will stop the eggs from cooking any further. If making the eggs ahead of time, remove them from the ice water and

CORNBREAD

1 cup semolina flour or cornmeal

1 cup all-purpose flour

¼ cup granulated sugar

2 tablespoons finely chopped
    fresh rosemary and/or sage

1 tablespoon baking powder

2 teaspoons kosher salt

½ teaspoon red pepper flakes,
    more if you're into spicy food

1 cup buttermilk

⅓ cup olive oil

4 tablespoons butter, melted

1 egg, room temperature

TOMATOES

12 Flavorino or Roma tomatoes,
    halved

3 tablespoons olive oil

2 tablespoons finely chopped
    fresh thyme

2 tablespoons finely chopped
    garlic

1 teaspoon kosher salt

WHERE TO FIND...

Pork
Truebridge Foods
Omaha, NE

Tomatoes
Shadow Brook Farm
Lincoln, NE

store them in their shells for up to 3 days in the refrigerator. If serving on the day you poach them, carefully remove each egg from its shell and place the egg into a bowl of cool water until you are ready to serve. To reheat the eggs, slide them into a pot of warm water for about 10 minutes. Use a slotted spoon to remove them from the warm water and serve.

TO MAKE THE CORNBREAD

Preheat the oven to 400°F.

In a large bowl, combine the dry ingredients.

In a medium bowl, combine the wet ingredients.

Add the wet ingredients to the dry ingredients and stir until well combined and no lumps are evident. Pour the mixture into a 9-inch, cast-iron pan and bake for 25 minutes, or until the cornbread is golden and a skewer comes out clean when placed into the center (leave the oven at 400°F to make the tomatoes). Set aside to cool for 20 minutes. Loosen the edges of the cornbread with a paring knife, turn out onto a plate, and let cool another 15 minutes. Cut into wedges.

TO MAKE THE TOMATOES

In a large bowl, coat the tomatoes with the other ingredients (olive oil through salt).

Place the tomatoes, cut side up, onto a baking sheet. Bake, uncovered, for about 45 minutes, or until softened and browned. When the tomatoes have 20 minutes left in the oven, cook the tesa.

TO COOK THE TESA AND ASSEMBLE THE DISH

You can cook tesa like bacon or like a ham "steak." The heat level varies depending on the desired result. If you want to serve the tesa like bacon, with the outside crispy, the fat rendered, and the meat cooked through, cut it into ¼-inch-thick slices and cook over low heat. If you want the tesa to have a ham-like texture, slice it ½ to ¾ inch thick. Cook the tesa over high heat on a hot pan to sear both sides quickly, then reduce the heat to medium to cook it through as desired (medium rare, medium, or well done). For all thicknesses, place the cooked tesa on a plate lined with paper towels to drain the fat.

On each of 4 plates, place a wedge of cornbread and a few slices of tesa. Add a spoonful of tomatoes and top with 2 eggs. Serve.

Note: There are some tesa recipes that call for the use of curing salt #1, also called pink salt, but I have found it is not necessary when curing pork belly for such a short time.

David Vetter

PRODUCER GRAIN PLACE FOODS | MARQUETTE, NE | GRAINPLACEFOODS.COM

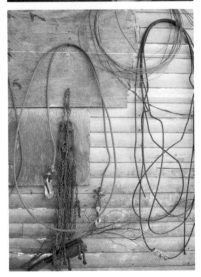

The Vetter family dedicated themselves to organic farming and manufacturing practices long before the word "organic" became part of our cultural nomenclature.

What started as a small family farm called The Grain Place has since blossomed into an international organic grain, legume, and seed processing facility known as Grain Place Foods. It was one of the first businesses in the region to provide small-scale organic growers with quality processing and distribution for organic whole grains. In Nebraska alone, it handles grains from 46 growers in 27 counties.

The road to this type of agriculture was slow, steady, and purposeful. It began in the 1940s when Don Vetter was one of the first farmers in Marquette to use post–World War II chemical farming practices. Enticed by the prospect of high yields and stable growth, he accepted this new, modern approach as the best way to manage and maintain the family farm. Within five years, however, he realized the drawbacks to chemical farming, and by 1953 Don became one of the earliest adopters of organic farming practices, despite the harsh scrutiny of his peers.

"My dad has always been an observant man. He's probably more observant than most. He spent his life in nature hunting and trapping. It's probably how he survived the 1930s," explains David, Don's eldest son. "So it didn't take too long for him to notice the impact that this new way of farming had on other species, crops, and the environment as a whole."

More than 20 years later, David worked with his dad to ensure organic certification for their 280-acre farm. The first parcel of land was certified organic in 1977, the remainder in 1978. It was one of the first certified farms in the region. Because this predated the US Department of Agriculture's interest in organic certification in the 1990s, and the 2002 National Organic Program labeling, Don and David made sure that the independent agencies they used were audited and reviewed in order to uphold certain standards.

Through David's experience in community agriculture, he soon learned that many families were seeking organic grain products. He and his father set out to test and research what would work well for the

In Nebraska alone, Grain Place Foods handles grains from 46 growers in 27 counties.

environmentally aware and health-conscious consumer. He also learned that many small organic growers were in need of a place they could trust.

Finally, during the farm crisis of the 1980s, the Vetters secured a bank loan at 18.9% interest to build a grain processing facility. It was a big risk during a tumultuous time. It wasn't until the early 1990s that they realized there was enough demand for high-quality organic grains, and they were in a position to meet it.

What began as an opportunity to help small organic growers like themselves has become the primary business for a family that has now ushered in its third generation—David's son, Madison, who serves as the warehouse manager. Where and how the business will evolve as the demand for organic products continues to increase has yet to be determined. For now, the Vetter men are happy to work together to bring quality grains to people everywhere. ∎

Black Walnut and Clove Muffins

SERVES 6–8

Black walnuts grow readily in Iowa and Nebraska. They have an intense, earthy flavor, making them a standout against their milder cousin, the English walnut. These muffins are perfect for an early summer morning, served warm with a pat of butter and homemade jam, or drizzled with honey.

—*Maggie Pleskac* MAGGIE'S VEGETARIAN CAFÉ | LINCOLN, NE

1¾ cups whole-wheat pastry flour or hard white-wheat flour

2 teaspoons baking powder

½ teaspoon sea salt

½ teaspoon ground cloves

1 cup black walnuts, chopped, divided

¾ cup granulated sugar

¾ cup whole milk

⅓ cup sunflower oil

2 eggs, room temperature

1 teaspoon vanilla extract

WHERE TO FIND...

Black Walnuts
Heartland Nuts 'N More
Valparaiso, NE

Hard White-Wheat Flour
Fehringer Farms
Sidney, NE

Milk
Prairieland Dairy
Firth, NE

Eggs
Common Good Farm
Raymond, NE

Oil
Bainter Sunflower Oil
Hoxie, KS

Preheat the oven to 350°F.

Sift the flour, baking powder, salt, and cloves together into a large bowl. Stir in ¾ cup of the walnuts. Set aside.

In a medium bowl, stir together the sugar, milk, oil, eggs, and vanilla until smooth. Add the wet ingredients to dry ingredients and stir until just combined. Do not overmix, or your muffins will turn into hockey pucks.

Line a muffin pan with paper muffin cups. Add a scant ½ cup of the batter into each paper cup. Garnish each muffin with the remaining walnuts.

Bake for 23 to 26 minutes, or until a toothpick comes out clean when inserted into the center of the muffin. Serve while still warm.

Caramelized Pattypan Squash Salad with Summer Peaches (p. 66)

Caramelized Pattypan Squash Salad with Summer Peaches

SERVES 8 (AS A SIDE DISH) OR 4 (AS A MAIN DISH) | PICTURED ON P. 65

This colorful dish comes together quickly and emphasizes the best of what the season has to offer. If you are pressed for time, leave out the green beans.

—Jason Simon ALBA | DES MOINES, IA

⅓ pound greens beans, stem ends removed

4 tablespoons olive oil, divided

24 small pattypan squash, sliced in half through stem

½ teaspoon kosher salt

¼ cup white wine

1 large yellow peach, cut into 16–20 slices

1 shallot, sliced paper thin

1 cup arugula

3 tablespoons fresh lemon juice (about 1 lemon)

Salt and freshly ground pepper, to taste

¼ cup shaved Grana Padano cheese or manchego cheese

WHERE TO FIND...

Pattypan Squash, Arugula
Cleverley Farms
Mingo, IA

Bring a medium pot of water to a boil. Fill a small bowl with ice water and set close by. Boil the green beans for about 4 minutes, until they are crisp-tender. They should be a bright green. Strain, then submerge the beans in the bowl of ice water to stop the cooking process. Once cool, drain the beans and set aside to dry on a dishtowel.

In a large sauté pan, heat 2 tablespoons of the oil over medium–high heat. Add the pattypan squash, cut side down, and the salt. You don't want to crowd the pan, so you may need to do this in batches. Cook until the cut side of the squash caramelizes and develops a deep brown color. Once all of the squash have browned, add them all back into the pan. Add the wine to deglaze. Sauté until the wine has evaporated. Remove the squash from the pan and let cool.

Using the same sauté pan, heat the remaining 2 tablespoons of the oil over medium heat. Add the peach segments and shallot slices and sauté until the shallots soften. Increase the heat to high, add the pattypan squash and green beans, and sauté for 1 minute. Remove from the heat and add the arugula and lemon juice. Season to taste with the salt and pepper. Divide onto plates and top each serving with some of the shaved Grana Padano cheese or manchego cheese. Serve warm.

Heirloom Tomato Panzanella

SERVES 8

A traditional dish served at room temperature, with many variations, panzanella is a great way to use up summer tomatoes and good crusty bread. It's also perfect for people like us, who use bread to crudely wipe the last drop of dressing from the salad bowl. It's best to make, serve, and eat this all in the same day.

—*Charlotte and John Hamburger* BACK ALLEY BAKERY | HASTINGS, NE

BREAD

6 cups cubed crusty white bread (1½-inch cubes)

¼ cup olive oil

¼ teaspoon kosher salt

5 twists of freshly ground black pepper

VINAIGRETTE

½ cup olive oil

3 tablespoons balsamic vinegar

2 teaspoons granulated sugar

2 cloves garlic, minced

½ teaspoon kosher salt

SALAD

4 large, ripe heirloom tomatoes, cored and cut into 1-inch cubes

1 cup sliced scallions, green and white parts

1 cup coarsely chopped fresh basil

WHERE TO FIND...

Tomatoes, Basil
26th Street Farm
Hastings, NE

TO MAKE THE BREAD

Preheat the oven to 350°F.

On a baking sheet, toss the bread cubes with the olive oil, salt, and pepper. Spread out in a single layer and bake the bread cubes in the oven until golden, about 20 minutes, stirring halfway through. Let the bread cool for 10 minutes before combining with the salad.

TO MAKE THE VINAIGRETTE

In a small bowl, whisk together the vinaigrette ingredients.

TO MAKE THE SALAD

In a large bowl, combine the salad ingredients. Pour the vinaigrette over the salad and toss. Add the toasted bread and toss again. Let sit at room temperature for 20 minutes before serving.

Paul Kulik

CHEF THE BOILER ROOM | 1110 JONES ST. | OMAHA, NE | 402.916.9274 |
WWW.BOILERROOMOMAHA.COM

Paul Kulik sits down on a black cushioned bar stool in the belly of The Boiler Room, one of his downtown Omaha restaurants. Soft morning light pours in through the giant windows of the upscale establishment, settling beneath industrial light fixtures that resemble glass juicers from the 1950s. Paul sips espresso at the bar as the light finds its way across his shoulders. He sets his cup down, rests on his forearms, and begins a three-hour interview explaining his philosophy of food in the Great Plains.

He is opinionated and unapologetic about the importance of local food, regional specialties, and the responsibility of chefs and restaurateurs to propel the movement forward.

"The Midwest at large, the Plains more specifically, have been utterly excluded from the conversation about food," he says. He pauses and ruminates for a moment on what he is about to say. "We've done a big part in excluding ourselves by refusing to update, by refusing to be part of the national dialogue."

As of late, however, the Great Plains have been receiving a bit more recognition, some of which can be attributed to the efforts made by Paul and his staff. By opening The Boiler Room in the winter of 2009, he challenged diners to expand both their palates and their concept of a regional dining experience.

Large images of animals in varying stages of repose hang on the dining room walls: a severed pig's head on a silver platter, a water fowl tucked neatly into a vase of flowers. Scenes such as these elevate the notion of knowing where your food comes from, especially when it's served

"We are building that rich tapestry of all the people it takes to have a complete food culture, which I would argue, right now, may be the most important expression of culture."

RECIPES FROM PAUL:

from a menu featuring local producers and food artfully created using French techniques.

As Paul finishes his drink, the morning speeds on. He speaks with his hands but rarely moves his shoulders. His blue eyes practically blaze when he discusses thick, tender asparagus; spicy radishes; and the delicate earthy sweetness of late winter or early spring Jerusalem artichokes.

"They taste better grown in Nebraska soil than anywhere else," he says. "The reason why I am in Omaha is the idea that we can do something really special within the region. We are building that rich tapestry of all the people it takes to have a complete food culture, which I would argue, right now, may be the most important expression of culture." ■

Heirloom Tomato Consommé

SERVES 10-12 (1 CUP PER PERSON)

Who doesn't like gazpacho? It is the quintessential summer soup. It's also entirely dependent on the quality of the tomatoes used. The same is true for consommé, a transparent, cold soup perfect for Nebraska's intense summer heat.

It takes three days for this soup to come together, but only 20 minutes of active time. A fleshy, low-seed, high-sugar, acidic tomato like Black Krim or Nebraska Wedding works well. Use the herbs you have available to make the bouquet; those listed here are some of my favorites. Espelette pepper provides a subtle, complex heat similar to a blend of paprika and cayenne pepper. You can find it online and in specialty spice shops.

—Paul Kulik THE BOILER ROOM | OMAHA, NE

8 sprigs fresh thyme

2 fresh bay leaves

1 sprig fresh rosemary

6 cups roughly chopped day-old crusty french bread

5 pounds heirloom tomatoes, roughly chopped

2½ medium yellow onions, roughly chopped

3 medium cucumbers, roughly chopped

½ head garlic, cloves peeled and crushed

2 tablespoons sel gris or kosher salt

¼ teaspoon ground Espelette pepper

Salt and freshly ground black pepper, to taste

Fresh chives, for garnish

Olive oil, for garnish

WHERE TO FIND...

Tomatoes
Shadow Brook Farm
Lincoln, NE

Tomatoes
Squeaky Greens Organics
Omaha, NE

Herbs, Onions
Blooms Organic
Crescent, IA

Tie the thyme, bay leaves, and rosemary together with string. Place the bundle into a 5-quart bowl.

Add the bread, tomatoes, onions, cucumbers, garlic, sel gris, and Espelette pepper to the bowl. Give the mixture a quick stir. Leave the bowl to stand at room temperature for 6 hours, then cover with plastic wrap and refrigerate overnight.

The next day, remove the herb bundle and thoroughly blend the remaining ingredients with an immersion blender, or in batches using a blender. Season to taste with the salt and pepper and store in the refrigerator for 2 days. The pulp should settle; the consommé is the clear liquid at the top, which you can spoon out. The pulp should be rather thick. You can discard it or use it as a wonderful addition to a Bloody Mary.

If the pulp doesn't settle, line a bowl with a generous amount of cheesecloth and pour half of the pulp into the cheesecloth. Place the bowl in your sink under the faucet. Tie the cheesecloth full of pulp to the faucet so it is suspended above the bowl. Repeat with the remaining pulp and hang from another location, such as the handle of a cupboard. The pulp will remain in the cloth, and the consommé will drip into the bowl. It will take about 4 hours for the consommé to drain from the pulp.

Ladle the consommé into individual bowls and garnish with a few clippings of fresh chives and a drizzle of olive oil.

George Formaro

CHEF CENTRO | 1003 LOCUST ST. | DES MOINES, IA | 515.248.1780 |
WWW.CENTRODESMOINES.COM

George Formaro's five Des Moines restaurants are built for volume, which he will admit makes sourcing local food in the quantities he needs a challenge. He typically buys a lot in season and uses food from local producers for dining specials and events. Although his restaurants, each of which has a different name and theme (including zombies), aren't considered seasonal establishments, his connection to garden-fresh food runs deep.

George spent summers pulling weeds and plucking tomatoes from the vines in his father's massive garden, then making sauces and pastas at his mother's side in the kitchen. His Italian American upbringing is how George absorbed not only the flavors of a heartfelt meal but also the healing power of a family dinner.

"Food brings people together. It has always been a way to bring people together. So when people come in for an anniversary, a first date, or even when they are sad, food is a way to feel better and to feel safe. There are a lot of things that go along with it. Food is always ground zero to me," he says on a Sunday afternoon while sitting at a corner table at Centro, his Italian-inspired eatery.

Tall, wide windows spill soft, natural light across midday diners visiting the restaurant, which is rich with history. Gray, black, and white hexagonal tiles—holdovers from the building's origins as a Masonic Temple—add a cozy touch to the immense space. Its neighbor, the artisan bread company South Union Bread Café, launched George's career both as a restaurateur and a chef.

He is a self-described shy guy, yet he could talk about food all day. In one breath he walks you through the details of nearly 3,000 cookbooks that line the walls of his basement, and in the next he shows the biggest wide-smiled enthusiasm over the intrinsic value of a 100-year-old recipe. He is not an intimidating person and doesn't want food to feel that way either. The flavor of corn, fresh from the farm, or a great-tasting slice of bread should be enough to spoil you; it doesn't need to be fussy.

"It just seems more natural to do what I've always done, which is to feed people using ingredients that were grown with passion," George says, donning his signature red bandana. "Most people who get behind a stove and cook professionally, they know that this is the way to do it." ∎

Sweet-Corn Chowder with Bacon and Sweet-Corn Salsa

SERVES 6 (1 ½ CUPS CHOWDER AND 3 TABLESPOONS SALSA PER PERSON)

One of my proudest moments as a chef was being asked to participate in a Niman Ranch Farmer Appreciation Dinner in Iowa. I paired bacon with sweet corn to make this luscious summer chowder. I served it hot, but it can be enjoyed at room temperature or cold just as easily.

—*George Formaro* CENTRO | DES MOINES, IA

SWEET-CORN SALSA

1 fresh poblano chile

2 large ears fresh sweet corn, kernels cut from the cob

1 large heirloom tomato (about ½ pound), seeded and chopped

3 tablespoons olive oil

2 tablespoons chopped red onion

2 tablespoons chopped fresh cilantro

2 teaspoons kosher salt

2 cloves garlic, minced

1 teaspoon red wine vinegar

½ teaspoon freshly ground black pepper

½ jalapeño chile, seeds and membrane removed, chopped

SWEET-CORN CHOWDER

4 cups chicken stock or vegetable stock

8 large ears sweet corn, kernels cut from cob (about 5½ cups)

1 small yellow onion, chopped (about ½ cup)

1 large clove garlic, chopped

2 sprigs fresh thyme

1½ cups heavy cream

5 tablespoons cornstarch

5 tablespoons cold water

Kosher salt and ground white pepper, to taste

10 slices bacon, cooked crisp and crumbled

WHERE TO FIND...

Sweet Corn	Tomato	Bacon
Grimes Sweet Corn	Cleverley Farms	Niman Ranch
Granger, IA	Mingo, IA	IA

TO MAKE THE SALSA

Preheat the broiler.

Place the poblano on a baking sheet and roast under the broiler for about 15 to 20 minutes. Using a pair of tongs, rotate the chile once the skin starts to blacken, about every 5 minutes. Remove from the oven, transfer to a bowl, cover with a dishtowel, and set aside to cool.

In a medium bowl, add the corn kernels, tomato, olive oil, onion, cilantro, salt, garlic, vinegar, black pepper, and jalapeño.

Once the poblano is cool to the touch, the blistered and blackened skin should pull off easily. Remove and discard the skin, seeds, and stem. Chop the poblano and add it to the bowl with the corn mixture. Stir, then refrigerate for 1 hour before serving.

TO MAKE THE CHOWDER

In a Dutch oven, bring the stock to a simmer over medium heat. Add the corn, onion, garlic, and thyme. Reduce the heat to low, cover, and simmer for 30 minutes.

Remove and discard the thyme. Purée approximately ½ of the chowder using an immersion blender, or in batches if using a blender, returning the puréed portion to the Dutch oven. Add the cream and bring the chowder to a simmer over low heat.

Mix the cornstarch and cold water together in a small cup, then add this mixture to the chowder while it is simmering. Stir to thicken. Season to taste with the salt and white pepper.

To serve, divide the chowder among bowls. Top each bowl with some of the corn salsa and crumbled bacon.

Note: Hot chilies like jalapeños and poblanos have oils that can remain on the skin even after washing. To prevent irritation, wear gloves or put a plastic bag over whichever hand is holding the chile.

Open-Faced Caponata and Heirloom Tomato Sandwich

SERVES 4

Caponata, a mixture of eggplant, onions, and tomatoes, is usually served as a salad or relish. It also, as in this recipe, makes an excellent sandwich. If you are hosting a party, triple the caponata and do it all a day or two before the big event.

If you are short on time, buy bread from your favorite bakery and whip this up for a simple weeknight meal.

The Mushroom Focaccia with Shallots, Savory, and Olive Oil (p. 112) works beautifully for this sandwich, with plenty left over for a rainy day (the recipe makes about 12 6 × 6-inch slices). Just omit the mushrooms.

—Benjamin Smart BIG GROVE BREWERY | SOLON, IA

1 large eggplant, diced

¼ cup plus 2 tablespoons olive oil, divided, plus more for brushing the focaccia

½ cup diced yellow onion

2 cloves garlic, minced

½ teaspoon red pepper flakes

1 tablespoon pine nuts

1 tablespoon dried currants or raisins

½ cup tomato purée

2 tablespoons balsamic vinegar

½ teaspoon dried thyme leaves

4 6 × 6-inch slices Mushroom Focaccia with Shallots, Savory, and Olive Oil (p. 112), made without mushrooms

2–3 large heirloom tomatoes, sliced thick

Fresh basil, for garnish

Shaved Parmigiano-Reggiano cheese, for garnish

WHERE TO FIND...

Eggplant, Tomatoes, Basil
Wild Woods Farm
Solon, IA

Preheat the oven to 375°F.

On a baking sheet, toss the eggplant with ¼ cup of the oil and roast until browned, 25 to 35 minutes.

In a large sauté pan, heat the remaining 2 tablespoons of the oil over medium heat. Add the onion and sauté until it is translucent. Add the garlic and red pepper flakes and cook 1 to 2 more minutes. Add the pine nuts and currants and stir to combine. Add the tomato purée, balsamic vinegar, thyme, and roasted eggplant. Bring to a simmer and cook for 5 minutes. Remove from the heat and let cool to room temperature.

Increase the oven temperature to 450°F.

Brush each slice of focaccia with some olive oil, and spoon the caponata on top. Place on a baking sheet and toast in the oven for about 5 minutes, until the focaccia is golden brown and crispy on the edges. Remove from the oven and top with the tomato slices. Garnish each sandwich with some of the basil and shaved Parmigiano-Reggiano. Eat immediately!

Michael Haskett

CHEF M.B. HASKETT DELICATESSEN | 324 S. PHILLIPS AVE. | SIOUX FALLS, SD | 605.367.1100 | MBHASKETT.COM

Michael Haskett stands behind the tallest part of his kitchen partition, wearing a black T-shirt and white apron. He's hunched over a cutting board, chopping bits of rhubarb and slicing strawberries, while his black thick-rimmed glasses creep slowly down his nose.

A stack of dishes awaits him, as do three customers sitting at the mismatched tables and one standing just inside the entrance waiting for a latte to go. They don't seem bothered by the wait; instead they are relaxing and enjoying a bit of conversation. Michael is one man down today, and like good neighbors and loyal diners, they understand.

In 2012, Michael and his father spent 16 days converting a friend's coffee shop into M.B. Haskett, a South Dakota delicatessen with schoolhouse pendant lights suspended from pressed-tin ceiling tiles. Since then, he has built a loyal following with an inspiring, ever-changing menu utilizing a limited kitchen: a few grills out back, a smoker, slow cookers, and a hot plate.

Now that he has proven his ability to survive in a world where restaurants can easily come and go within a year, he is eager to renovate the building and cook with a hood and full stove, items generally considered essential kitchen tools for most restaurants.

The menu changes according to seasonal availability and his mood. During the summer months, he uses most of the food from his own garden and supplements it with local producers. Menu offerings include creative nods to Italian, Mediterranean, local, and Mexican cuisine. His anything-goes approach to menu planning mimics his anything-went approach to his culinary training and pre-restaurateur status.

"When I was 19 one of my mentors said, 'Don't ever spend more than 12 months at a place. You need to get out there and see the different ways of doing things.' That really guided me," Michael says.

After high school he left South Dakota to pursue an education at the Culinary Institute of America in Hyde Park, New York. From there he bounced around Seattle, Washington; Minnesota; Colorado; and even Japan for a bit. In the end, however, he rekindled his love for the state he called home and put down roots in South Dakota.

He was motivated by civic pride and his desire to be a change agent. The culinary landscape, according to Michael, was virtually untapped in Sioux Falls. Moving home provided him with the opportunity to promote a local food culture where ingredients were expertly grown and meals were thoughtfully prepared. He wanted a clear line of demarcation between his establishment and the heat-and-serve chain restaurants he worked at in his youth.

"I have tons of South Dakota pride," he says as he walks out from behind the counter to deliver the last sandwich order. "We are an agricultural state and there is no reason why we can't take just a couple of handfuls of acres here and there, put hoop houses on them, and grow produce—really good produce."

As the afternoon wears on, the dishes pile higher, and customers delight in their sandwiches, quiche, and coffee drinks. They ask about the prix fixe menu for the weekend and confirm standing reservations. One even hops behind the counter to wash a few plates and help Michael get set up for dinner service. It's clear the place belongs to all who enter, and that Michael has earned their respect by feeding them well. ■

Walleye Tacos with Charred Salsa

SERVES 6 (2 TACOS PER PERSON)

I've rarely met a person who didn't like a taco, and since a chef and mentor in the Twin Cities taught me the authentic method for these Mexican staples, it's hard to be satisfied with anything less.

We don't have a stove at the restaurant, so we get creative with how we use the grill—like for boiling water and panfrying. When the tomatoes ripen and the fish are biting at the lake, then you know it's time to fire up the coals.

—*Michael Haskett* M.B. HASKETT DELICATESSEN | SIOUX FALLS, SD

CHARRED SALSA AND TACO TOPPINGS

3 large, ripe tomatoes

1 red bell pepper

1 green bell pepper

2 jalapeño chilies

1 small yellow onion

1 head garlic (skin on)

2 bunches fresh cilantro, chopped, divided

2½ limes, divided

½ lemon

½ orange

Salt, to taste

1 small head cabbage, thinly sliced into ribbons, for topping

1 cup crumbled cotija cheese, for topping

2 avocados, sliced, for topping

TACOS

2 pounds walleye fillets, skinned, pin bones removed

½ cup cornmeal

¼ cup all-purpose flour

1 tablespoon ground paprika

2 teaspoons salt

1 teaspoon ground cayenne pepper

1 cup heavy cream

Grapeseed oil, for panfrying

12 small corn tortillas

TO MAKE THE SALSA AND PREPARE THE TOPPINGS

On your outdoor grill, start a good amount of charcoal (or, if it's gas, just fire it up). You are going to roast the vegetables whole over the flames, so you want the grill good and hot.

Cut just the root end off of the onion so it stays intact while roasting.

When the coals are white hot or your gas grill reaches 375°F, place the whole tomatoes, peppers, onion, and garlic directly into the coals with long tongs (or, for a gas grill, over the flames but still on the grill plate). Turn the vegetables about every 45 seconds, until the skins are black and blistered. The tomatoes and peppers can come off the grill after about 2 to 3 minutes. Place them in a large mixing bowl. Follow them with the onion and then the garlic, which should remain on the grill the longest. Cover the bowl with plastic wrap to let the residual heat continue to work on the peppers and onion.

Once the vegetables cool down a bit, you should be able to pull the skins off easily with your fingers. Remove the skins from the peppers and onion. A little of the char is OK to leave on. For spicy salsa, leave the seeds in the jalapeños; for mild salsa, remove and discard the seeds, or omit the jalapeños entirely.

Roughly chop the tomatoes, peppers, and onion, and return them to the bowl. Remove the paper skin from the garlic and discard. Mince the garlic and add it to the bowl. Add the chopped cilantro leaves and about ½ of the stems from 1 bunch. In a small bowl, zest 1 of the limes; set the zest and ½ of the lime aside (you will use it for the fish batter). Add the juice from the other ½ of the lime, ½ of the lemon, and ½ of the orange to the salsa. Stir to combine. Add salt, a little at a time, until you think it's appropriately seasoned. This is my favorite part, but it can lead to about half of the salsa being eaten before it's served. A night in the fridge makes this salsa even better.

Cut 1½ limes into wedges. On a serving platter, arrange the lime wedges, remaining cilantro, cabbage, and cotija cheese. Save room on the platter for a bowl of the salsa and for the avocados, which should be cut immediately before serving.

TO MAKE THE TACOS

Cut the fillets on the bias into strips about 1 inch thick by about 2 to 3 inches long and set aside. Line a platter with paper towels and set aside.

In a medium shallow dish, combine the cornmeal, flour, paprika, salt, cayenne pepper, and lime zest reserved from making the salsa. Set aside.

In a small bowl, juice the remaining ½ of a lime. Set aside.

In a large cup, combine the heavy cream with 1 tablespoon of the reserved lime juice. Let thicken for 5 minutes. Give it a quick stir, then pour it into a shallow bowl.

On your grill or stovetop, heat a large (12-inch) sauté pan. If you are working on the grill, use a cast-iron pan. Add enough oil to cover about a ½- to ¾-inch depth.

While you wait for the oil to heat, start breading your fish. Coat it in the cream mixture, let the excess drip off, then dredge it in the cornmeal mixture. Let it sit for about 5 minutes so the crust adheres better to the fish. Do this with all the fish.

After about 5 minutes, sprinkle a pinch of the cornmeal mixture into the oil. If it sputters, the oil is ready. Add the fish in small batches so the temperature of the cast-iron pan stays hot and you can manage turning the fish. It shouldn't take more than a few minutes per side, depending on the thickness of the strips. Flip the fish as needed, and when cooked through, remove from the pan and place on the prepared platter to drain the excess oil.

If you are frying the fish on the grill, toast some corn tortillas by placing them in stacks of 2 directly over the coals, flipping once so that the inside steams soft and the outside is lightly blistered black. It takes about 30 to 45 seconds per side, depending on the heat of the grill. Transfer the tortillas to a platter. You want each person to have 2 tortillas.

Transfer the fish to a clean platter. Set this alongside the toppings, salsa, and tortillas. Enjoy outside—preferably near the lake where you caught the fish.

WHERE TO FIND...

Cabbage, Cilantro, Peppers, Tomatoes, Onion
Linda's Gardens
Chester, SD

Garlic
Prairie Coteau Farm
Astoria, SD

Walleye
Your Favorite Lake
Anywhere

Kevin Loth and Charuth van Beuzekom

FARMERS AND ARTISANS SHADOW BROOK FARM AND DUTCH GIRL CREAMERY | LINCOLN, NE | WWW.SHADOWBRK.COM

Charuth van Beuzekom stands in a field of chicory, birdsfoot trefoil, and timothy. Her tiny five-foot-five-inch frame looks comfortable and content among a sea of ivory, brown, and charcoal goats nibbling on the grasses and prairie flowers at her feet.

"Come girls; come girls!" she calls, to bring them in from the pasture.

She and her husband, Kevin Loth, are farmers' market mainstays. They have been selling baskets of sprouts and looming lengths of delphinium, larkspur, and snapdragon at the southeast corner of the downtown Omaha Farmers Market for 20 years. As seasons became decades, their family grew to include three sons, and their organic vegetable and flower farm, Shadow Brook, has grown to include a construction business as well as a goat-dairy operation called Dutch Girl Creamery.

"We were that cute couple at the farmers' market with a baby strapped to our back selling salad mix," she says, reminiscing about their idealistic beginnings as young farmers.

Today, as it was back then, morning market goers adorned with canvas bags wait for the opening bell to ring, poised and ready to buy the

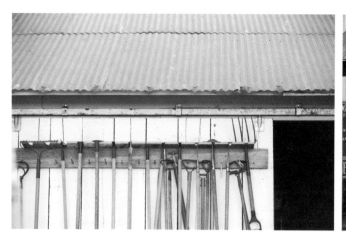

During their first years at the market, Charuth and Kevin were happy to sell a modest 10 to 30 pounds of salad mix per week; now they sell 500 pounds per week.

week's weight in greens and sunflower sprouts. During their first years at the market, Charuth and Kevin were happy to sell a modest 10 to 30 pounds of salad mix per week; now they sell 500 pounds per week.

In 2006, they formally launched Dutch Girl Creamery, which is one of only five goat dairies in Nebraska and one of only two on the state's eastern side. Charuth milks her own herd of 100 goats; she uses the milk to create yogurt, goat cheese truffles, and specialty cheeses all named after women.

"I call the cheeses my daughters, because my actual children are all boys," she says with a smile. "What's the point if you aren't going to have a little fun?"

We walk the driveway sparsely covered with limestone toward the big, white, wide-mouthed barn as chickens meander and peck their way across our path like a group of stumbling drunks. Nearby, a few rambunctious goats are climbing a nearly dead tree; finally one prevails and claims its spot above the others in the stripped branches.

"How could a person not enjoy working with goats?" Charuth says. "They are always doing something that makes you laugh."

Kevin walks by on his way to tend to fields down the road as Charuth reaches the barn. Inside, tiny, energetic goats climb pallets of organic feed four feet high and leap off to tackle their cohorts—it's a vision of joy and child-like play. ■

Ricotta Gnocchi with Heirloom Tomato Marmalade

SERVES 4 (WITH EXTRA GNOCCHI FOR FREEZING)

Summer is rich with heirloom tomatoes, and once they're off the vine, the window of time in which you can use them is short. This recipe should be started the day before you plan to serve it, as the ricotta must strain overnight. You will have extra gnocchi, which freeze well, so feel free to save some for a quick and easy weeknight meal. The tomato marmalade beautifully captures the essence of the season. The hour it takes the marmalade to come together is well worth the wait. Lancaster Duet is a silky, creamy, aged, washed-rind cheese made from a combination of cow and goat milk.

—*Clayton Chapman* THE GREY PLUME | OMAHA, NE

HOMEMADE RICOTTA

1 gallon whole milk

¾ cup fresh lemon juice (about 3 or 4 lemons)

RICOTTA GNOCCHI

Homemade Ricotta

1 egg

1 egg yolk

1½ teaspoons olive oil

Zest of 1 lemon, plus more for garnish

1 scant teaspoon kosher salt

1½–2 cups all-purpose flour or hard white-wheat flour, plus more as needed to form dough

TOMATO MARMALADE AND FINISHING SAUCE

2 pounds heirloom tomatoes, various colors, plus 2 tomatoes, for plating

2 shallots, minced

2 tablespoons granulated or raw sugar

2 tablespoons olive oil

1 clove garlic, minced

3 sprigs fresh thyme

½ teaspoon kosher salt, or to taste

½ cup shaved Lancaster Duet cheese, divided

1 tablespoon minced fresh basil or chives

Salt and freshly ground black pepper, to taste

¼ pound arugula

2½ tablespoons crème fraîche or sour cream

2 tablespoons unsalted butter

TO MAKE THE RICOTTA

In a large, nonreactive pot over medium heat, combine the milk and lemon juice. The milk will start to slowly form curds over the course of 1 to 1½ hours or so. Be patient and don't turn up the heat. The curds are much creamier when formed slowly. Do not stir.

Meanwhile, line a fine-mesh strainer with cheesecloth and set it over a bowl. Once all of the curds have risen to the top, and the rest of the liquid looks like yellow water, remove the pot from the heat and skim the curds off of the top, placing them in the prepared strainer. Let the cheese drain overnight in the refrigerator with a plate on top. It will yield approximately 1 pound of cheese. The cheese will be soft, moist, and slightly crumbly.

Continued

TO MAKE THE GNOCCHI

In a large bowl, combine the ricotta, egg, egg yolk, olive oil, lemon zest, and salt. Slowly incorporate the flour with a rubber spatula until the dough is firm enough to handle, but still very soft. Start with 1½ cups of flour and add more as needed; you probably won't use more than about 2 cups.

Once the dough is formed, separate the dough into approximately 100 tiny spheres that are the size of a nickel (or quarter if you prefer). Place a fork on your work surface tine-side down, so the back of the fork is facing you. Place the dough spheres on the back of the fork and indent them with your thumb. Peel them off the fork and tuck into a football shape. Lines from the fork tines will be on one side, and lines where the gnocchi came together will be on the other side.

TO MAKE THE TOMATO MARMALADE AND ASSEMBLE THE DISH

Bring a large pot of water to a boil. With a paring knife, score an *X* in the bottom of 2 pounds' worth of tomatoes. Blanch the tomatoes in the boiling water for about 10 seconds. Remove from the water. Peel off the skin and discard, and remove and discard the seeds. Dice the tomato flesh into about a ¼-inch dice.

In another large pot (or the same pot that you've rinsed out), combine the diced tomatoes, shallots, sugar, olive oil, garlic, thyme, and salt. Bring to a boil, then reduce the heat to medium and cook for 45 to 60 minutes, or until most of the water is evaporated and the tomatoes have absorbed the oil. They will be soft and shiny from absorbing the olive oil. Remove and discard the thyme sprigs. Fold in ¼ cup of the Lancaster Duet cheese and the basil. Set aside until ready to serve.

Thinly slice the remaining 2 tomatoes. Place 2 slices on the base of each of 4 plates. Sprinkle with the salt and pepper. Top each plate with some arugula leaves and set aside.

Bring a large pot of water to a boil. Count out 40 gnocchi (about 10 per person) and drop them in the water. Cook the gnocchi until they float, about 1 minute. Drain.

In a large sauté pan, combine the crème fraîche and butter and bring to a simmer. Add the cooked gnocchi and tomato marmalade. Sauté until everything is warmed through. On each plate, place a pile of gnocchi and marmalade on top of the raw tomatoes and arugula. Garnish with the remaining ¼ cup of the cheese and some lemon zest. Serve.

Tomato Chutney

MAKES 2 CUPS

Chutney is a wonderfully versatile condiment. Use it for crostini with a smear of goat cheese, spoon a little over grilled chicken, or use it to top your next burger instead of ketchup.

—*Sean Wilson* PROOF | DES MOINES, IA

2 pounds tomatoes

¼ cup white vinegar

2 cloves garlic

1 1-inch piece ginger root, peeled

½ onion, chopped

1 jalapeño chile, seeded and minced

½ cup brown sugar

½ teaspoon salt

¼ cup golden raisins

2 tablespoons chopped and toasted pecans

½ teaspoon lemon zest

WHERE TO FIND...

Tomatoes
Butcher Crick Farms
Carlisle, IA

Garlic
Grade A Gardens
Johnston, IA

Bring a large pot of water to a boil. With a paring knife, score an *X* in the bottom of your tomatoes. Place them in the pot of boiling water for about 30 seconds. Peel off the skin and discard, and remove and discard the cores. Chop the tomatoes, then set aside.

In a blender, purée the vinegar, garlic, and ginger.

In a medium saucepan, sauté the onion over medium–low heat, until soft. Add the garlic purée, tomatoes, jalapeño, sugar, and salt and bring to a boil. Reduce the heat and simmer, uncovered, stirring frequently, until nearly all the liquid is absorbed, about 45 minutes to 1 hour. Stir in the raisins, pecans, and lemon zest. Cook for a few more minutes. Remove from the heat and let cool. Store the chutney in an airtight container in the refrigerator for up to 1 week.

Doug and Krista Dittman

FARMERS AND ARTISANS BRANCHED OAK FARM | RAYMOND, NE | BRANCHEDOAKFARM.COM

The sun rises softly over bur oak trees heavy with bright-green acorns. Their gnarled branches and deeply grooved trunks pepper the rolling pastures at Branched Oak Farm.

In the distance, Doug Dittman, a practicing Buddhist and dairy farmer, carefully drives 20 head of cattle from the pasture slowly across a ridge and into the milking room. A John Deere tractor sits idle while the tan-and-oatmeal-colored Jersey cows are readied to provide milk for Branched Oak cheese.

Krista Dittman emerges from the family's deep-red stucco and stone home to greet me. She has a calm and composed way about her—a stillness that flows through the fiber of the 240-acre farm, which includes her cheese-production facility. The land has been in Doug's family for three generations, although until recently, farming wasn't a family business. Doug's interest in nature and the environment led him and Krista to move to Raymond and eventually give up careers in academia to build a life as farmers, cheesemakers, and lovers of good food.

"The cheese we create is unique," Doug says during a recent outdoor dinner event at the farm. "It can only come from this place, at this time, from these people. You are eating cheese that comes from a place."

> *"The cheese we create is unique. It can only come from this place, at this time, from these people."*

The high butterfat content of the milk and the distinctive flavors of their grass-fed herd create a taste profile reflective of the region. This idea of *place* in both taste and geography is becoming more and more important, both for food lovers as well as those who simply seek authentic flavor experiences in our evermore homogenized world. Krista's craftsmanship yields fresh, tangy, creamy, pungent, and hard-rind cheeses worthy of the national attention she receives in print and at white-tablecloth restaurants and specialty shops throughout the United States.

Coming into their current roles as dairyman and cheesemaker wasn't immediate. The farm and the Dittmans lived through many incarnations

before focusing on their current efforts as a dairy. They tried their hands at beef cattle, produce, and eggs before seeing milk and cheese as their strongest and most interesting opportunity. From the outside, the risk seemed big, considering dairy farming in Nebraska is a dwindling industry. In 1996, the state had 1,044 dairy farms, and in less than 20 years the number has fallen to 187. Krista, however, realized the dairy's success would come from specialty cheese production rather than liquid-milk sales.

"Food motivates me," she says while spooning dollop after dollop of creamy, tangy Quark, a fresh European-style cheese, into a ramekin. "It all comes back to food. I love to cook. I love to eat. I love it to taste good. I feel like I'm sustained physiologically and psychologically when I know where it comes from, and I want to share the experience of joy that comes from eating well."

She offers me a smear of Quark followed by a slice of Black Jack, a pepper-coated, young jack cheese. She does the same for herself. She samples and savors slivers and segments of one cheese after another. She explains the qualities of each while considering the tastes and textures, like an artist examining a recently finished painting, and then, as if she were thinking to herself, "This turned out just right," a gentle smile breaks the concentration on her face, and with a self-affirming nod, she gives herself permission to move on with her day. ∎

Toast with Homemade Ricotta and Fresh Strawberry Jam

SERVES 12 (2 TOASTS PER PERSON; JAM MAKES ABOUT 2 ¼ CUPS; RICOTTA MAKES ABOUT 4½ CUPS)

A little planning is required for this dish, because the ricotta has to drain overnight. Once you get started, however, you will realize how easy it is to make your own. This simple and delicious treat can be shared and served in many ways. Spread some savory ricotta on crusty bread and top with a quick and flavorful strawberry jam, as I have it here, or drizzle with olive oil and top with arugula. This versatile dish can be served to a group with breakfast, or as an appetizer or after-dinner dessert. I like to enjoy it outside with those I love, while watching the sun go down and sipping a chilled, crisp glass of my favorite white wine.

—Nick Strawhecker DANTE RISTORANTE PIZZERIA | OMAHA, NE

HOMEMADE RICOTTA

½ gallon whole milk

1 pint half-and-half

1 pint heavy cream

1 pint buttermilk

⅔ cup fresh lemon juice (about 4 lemons)

2 tablespoons white balsamic vinegar

¼ cup finely grated Grana Padano cheese or Parmigiano-Reggiano cheese

2 tablespoons olive oil

Salt and freshly ground black pepper, to taste

JAM

2 pounds strawberries, hulled and roughly chopped (most any other fruit will also work)

2 cups granulated sugar

2 tablespoons fresh lemon juice

TOAST

1 loaf crusty bread

Olive oil, for brushing

WHERE TO FIND...

Milk
Branched Oak Farm
Raymond, NE

TO MAKE THE RICOTTA

Layer several pieces of cheesecloth into a large fine-mesh strainer. Place over a large bowl. Set aside.

In a large pot, combine all the dairy ingredients and warm over medium heat. When the mixture reaches 185°F, add the lemon juice and vinegar. When the temperature reaches 195°F, remove from the heat and pour the mixture into the prepared strainer. Discard the liquid in the bowl. Place the strainer back over the now-empty bowl and let the ricotta drain in the refrigerator overnight. The next day, remove the ricotta from the refrigerator and transfer to a mixing bowl. Add the grated cheese and olive oil, and season to taste with the salt and pepper. Mix well.

TO MAKE THE JAM AND TOAST

In a large, heavy-bottomed saucepan over high heat, combine the strawberries, sugar, and lemon juice. Make sure there is plenty of room in the saucepan, as the jam will need room to expand and foam.

Bring the mixture to a hard boil for about 45 minutes to 1 hour, stirring frequently. Cool.

Preheat the oven to 350°F.

Cut the bread on the bias into 24 slices. Brush the slices with the olive oil and toast in the oven for 10 to 15 minutes. You can put the slices on a baking sheet or directly on the oven racks; it's up to you.

Remove the toast from the oven and spread 2 heaping tablespoons of ricotta on each slice. Top with 1 teaspoon of jam. Of course, these are just suggestions. If you want to use more ricotta or more jam, feel free to indulge. The jam will keep in the refrigerator for about 7 days; the ricotta will keep in the refrigerator for about 5 days.

Sweet-Corn Custard with Ground Cherries

SERVES 6

One of the flavors I look forward to most in the high summer of Nebraska is our golden-yellow, juicy, sugary sweet corn. Since my childhood, there has been many a July meal made of nothing more than some sliced tomato and several ears of roasted sweet corn slathered in butter. I buy it from Greg Naber of Naber's Produce in York. The quality and consistency of his corn is always high. Ground cherries, sometimes called cape gooseberries, are sweet, golden orbs that grow inside of paper husks.

This recipe involves a little extra preparation time, but if you find pleasure in the process like I do, the added effort increases the joy of this dish. The ratio is simple and the outcome is outstanding. It is made without milk, which is good news for those with allergies to dairy.

—*Kevin Shinn* BREAD AND CUP | LINCOLN, NE

8–12 ears sweet corn

1 cup eggs (about 4 eggs)

¾ cup granulated sugar

¼ teaspoon vanilla extract

1 package ground cherries or other seasonal berry (about 24 ground cherries or ½ pint berries)

WHERE TO FIND...

Corn
Naber's Produce
York, NE

Ground Cherries
Squeaky Green Organics
Omaha, NE

Preheat the oven to 350°F.

Cut the kernels from the cobs of fresh, uncooked sweet corn. Set the kernels aside.

One by one, hold a cob over a medium bowl and scrape it with the back of your knife to release the rest of the corn juice. Set aside.

Layer cheesecloth over a fine-mesh strainer. Leave some cloth hanging over the sides so you can wrap and twist it later. Place the strainer over the bowl of corn juice.

In your food processor fitted with the S blade, process the corn kernels in batches until the consistency is a fine pulp. Pour the corn pulp and any juice into the prepared strainer. Pull up the sides of the cheesecloth, making sure the pulp is fully contained, and twist to squeeze out the juice, until you get 2 cups. Discard the pulp.

Add the eggs, sugar, and vanilla extract to the corn juice and, using a blender or an immersion blender, mix until fully combined and just beginning to froth.

Evenly distribute the custard into 6 3-inch ramekins. Place the ramekins in a 9 × 13-inch cake pan. Slowly add very hot water to the pan, until water reaches the middle of the ramekins. This bain-marie will help the custard bake more evenly and gently.

Bake for 20 to 22 minutes. The custard will puff up toward the end of the baking. Your custard is ready when a toothpick inserted in the center comes out clean. Carefully remove the pan from the oven, as the water in the pan will be very hot. Slowly and carefully lift the ramekins out of the water and set aside to cool for 30 minutes. Garnish each custard with 3 or 4 ground cherries, leaving 1 or 2 in their husks, or use any summer fruit, such as blackberries or raspberries, or even a spoonful of raw sweet-corn kernels.

24K Carrot Cake with Cream Cheese Frosting

SERVES 8

This cake is the best way to eat your vegetables. Store leftovers in the refrigerator, but bring to room temperature before serving.

—*Kristine Moberg* QUEEN CITY BAKERY | SIOUX FALLS, SD

CAKE

2½ cups all-purpose flour

1½ teaspoons ground cinnamon

1¼ teaspoons baking powder

1 teaspoon baking soda

¼ teaspoon ground nutmeg

⅛ teaspoon ground cloves

1¾ cups granulated sugar

½ teaspoon kosher salt

½ teaspoon orange zest

1½ cups sunflower oil

4 eggs

4½ cups grated carrots

½ cup shredded sweetened coconut

¼ cup crushed and drained canned pineapple

ICING

1 cup unsalted butter, softened

1 pound cream cheese, softened

1 tablespoon vanilla extract

12 ounces confectioners' sugar, sifted

WHERE TO FIND...

Carrots
The Cornucopia
Sioux Center, IA

Dairy
Burbach's Countryside Dairy
Hartington, NE

TO MAKE THE CAKE

Preheat the oven to 350°F.

Butter 3 8-inch round cake pans, then cut out a circle of parchment paper to cover the bottom of each.

In a medium bowl, sift together the flour, cinnamon, baking powder, baking soda, nutmeg, and cloves and set aside.

In a large bowl, whisk together the sugar, salt, and orange zest. Whisk in the oil and eggs until well combined. Using a spoon or stiff spatula, add the carrots, coconut, and pineapple; stir until combined. Gently fold the dry ingredients into the wet. Do not overmix, as doing so will result in a tough cake.

Pour a scant 2¼ cups of cake batter into each prepared pan. Bake for 25 minutes, or until a toothpick inserted in the center comes out clean. Cool completely before removing from the pans.

TO MAKE THE ICING

In the bowl of a stand mixer fitted with the paddle attachment, cream the butter until it is smooth and has absolutely no lumps, about 1 to 2 minutes. Scrape down the bowl; add the cream cheese and cream until combined. Scrape down the bowl. Add the vanilla extract and mix again. Scrape down the bowl. With the mixer running, gradually add the confectioners' sugar. Scrape down the bowl, then mix for about 2 more minutes. Be careful not to overmix, as the icing will lose its structure.

Place 1 cake layer on a cake stand. Spread some icing on top of the first layer. Place the second layer of cake on top of the first and top that layer with icing as well. Place the third layer of cake upside down on the second; this will give you a nice level top to your cake. Plop quite a bit of icing on the top and, using an offset spatula, work the icing out to the sides in a circular motion. It's OK if icing hangs over the sides of the cake. Continue working the icing over the top and down the sides of the cake. Finally, smooth out the sides and add more icing if needed. Serve. As mentioned above, you can also refrigerate the cake if you want to serve it later—just make sure to serve at room temperature.

Fall

Charlotte and John Hamburger

BAKERS BACK ALLEY BAKERY | 609 W. 2ND ST. | HASTINGS, NE |
402.460.5056 | WWW.BACKALLEYBAKERY.COM

Charlotte and John Hamburger started Back Alley Bakery by accident.

John, a construction contractor by trade, challenged a friend to see who could bake the best loaf of bread. Using the back room of an old building, the two men built a wood-fired brick oven. Within months, people heard about the underground baking project and lined up from the back-alley door down the block.

Eventually, the two friends ditched the competition and spent most of 2003 perfecting their recipes and giving away 200 loaves of bread every weekend. Once confident in their bread-making abilities, they used the mailing list they had built over the previous 12 months to sell their loaves of crusty, rustic sourdough from the same back door.

After nearly six years of selling bread through the alley, Back Alley expanded through to the street when the tenant in the front of the building closed its doors. John's partner withdrew from the bread business to focus his attention on his architectural firm, and Back Alley Bakery became a Hamburger family business. John's wife, Charlotte, joined forces with their daughter, Ellen, to become the cook and pastry chef, respectively.

John continues to run the family construction business Monday through Friday, but on Saturday mornings around two you will find him at the bakery. It is in the predawn hours that he is most at peace, checking the oven and working with wild sourdough cultures and organic grains to make crusty, carbohydrate-laden rounds and ovals so substantial that using a knife to cut them, rather than tearing chunks off with your bare hands, would be an insult.

"We don't use commercial yeast. We use sourdough cultures from the earth. It's more natural that way and I think it's a better process all the way around."

"We don't use commercial yeast. We use sourdough cultures from the earth. It's more natural that way and I think it's a better process all

the way around. Natural cultures have their own rules and you have to live with it. It makes things more difficult, but also makes it more interesting," says John.

In addition to wild starters and local organic grains, John, Charlotte, and their team use produce, eggs, and honey from local farmers to create everything from soup to pizza.

For Charlotte, making quality food and serving it to her community is an expression of love. "I really think it makes a difference how the cooks are feeling when they prepare the food," she says. "We try to keep things wholesome and prepare the food in a loving way. I think because of that we've been more successful than we've ever dreamed." ■

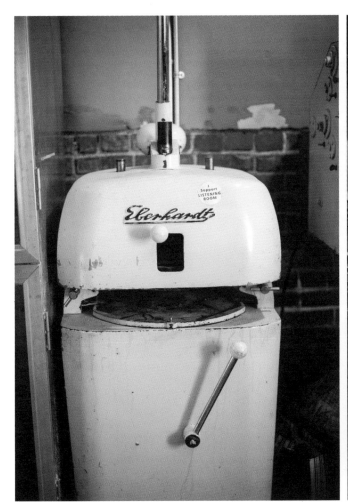

Honey–Oat Bread (p. 110)

Honey–Oat Bread

MAKES 2 LOAVES | PICTURED ON P. 109

At the bakery we use wild starter, but you can also use packaged yeast and it will work just as well. This barely sweet but robust bread is perfect with salads, or on its own spread with butter and honey.

—Charlotte and John Hamburger BACK ALLEY BAKERY | HASTINGS, NE

Unsalted butter, for greasing

1 ¼-ounce package active dry yeast or 1 cup Wild Yeast Starter (recipe follows)

2 cups warm water (100°F–115°F), divided, plus more for cake pan

2 cups rolled oats, divided

1½ cups hard red-wheat flour

¼ cup honey

¼ cup blackstrap molasses

1½ teaspoons fine sea salt

3½–4 cups unbleached, unbro-mated, white all-purpose flour, plus extra for kneading

Cornmeal, for dusting

WHERE TO FIND...

Honey
Walnut Creek Organic Ranch
Deweese, NE

Rolled Oats,
Hard Red-Wheat Flour
Grain Place Foods
Marquette, NE

Grease a large bowl with the butter and set aside.

Mix the yeast into 1 cup of the warm water and let the mixture stand for 10 minutes. Make sure the water is between 100°F and 115°F. If the water is too hot, it will kill the yeast and your bread will fail to rise. If you are using the Wild Yeast Starter instead of packaged yeast, scoop out 1 cup of starter and place it in a medium bowl.

In a separate large bowl, slowly combine the remaining 1 cup of warm water with 1½ cups of the rolled oats and the wheat flour, honey, molasses, and salt. Add the yeast mixture. Once combined, slowly stir in about 3 cups of the all-purpose flour. Add the remaining 1 cup of flour little by little, until the dough becomes too dry to stir. You may not use all of the flour.

Turn the dough out onto a floured work surface and knead with the remaining all-purpose flour, adding more flour if you used it all previously, until the dough is glistening and elastic. Don't overdo the flour—hydration is good. Transfer the dough into the prepared, buttered bowl; cover with plastic wrap; and set in a warm place for 2 hours or so, until the dough has doubled in size. A spot on the countertop where the sun shines is the perfect place.

Dust a baking sheet with the cornmeal and set aside.

Once the dough has doubled, turn it out onto a lightly floured work surface. Divide the dough in half. If the dough is sticky, use a little flour just until it no longer sticks. Shape each half into an oval loaf. Place on the prepared baking sheet. Cover with a lightweight towel and let the loaves rise in a warm place (75°F to 80°F) until the dough nearly doubles in size again. This should take about an additional 2 hours.

You can bake the loaves on 1 of 3 surfaces. If you have a baking tile or clay cloche, use it according to the manufacturer's recommendations. If not, a pizza stone is a great substitute. Place the tile, cloche, or pizza stone on the middle rack in the oven. Fill a cake pan ⅓ of the way with water and place it on the rack below the tile, cloche, or pizza stone.

Preheat the oven to 450°F. You want the baking surface to warm up before placing the bread on it. The water in the cake pan will create a steam bath for the bread, resulting in a crust that will snap.

While the oven is warming, lightly wet the top of the bread with a spray bottle of water or pastry brush, and sprinkle the loaves liberally with the remaining ½ cup of rolled oats. Wet again. Using a sharp knife or razor blade, make 3 cuts about ¼ inch deep, at an angle, across the top of the bread. Place the loaves in the oven on the hot tile, cloche, or pizza stone.

Bake for 20 minutes, then reduce the oven heat to 350°F and bake for another 17 to 20 minutes, until the loaf sounds hollow when the bottom is slapped. Cool before serving.

Wild Yeast Starter

2 cups all-purpose flour, divided
2 cups water, divided

Mix 1 cup each of the flour and water together and cover with a clean cloth or fine-mesh strainer. Set near an open window. Watch your bowl for signs of activity. Within 3 days, you should see bubbling, indicating that you have captured some wild yeast. When this happens, dump out ½ of the mixture and stir into the remaining mixture another ½ cup of the water and ½ cup of the flour. Let sit 1 more day, and then repeat the dumping and adding. When the mixture is bubbling nicely after 1 more day, it is ready to produce bread for you.

Use 1 cup of this yeast starter to replace the active dry yeast and 1 cup of the water in the bread recipe.

Mushroom Focaccia with Shallots, Savory, and Olive Oil

SERVES 12

This chewy, tender flatbread is best to make on a Saturday when you're stuck at home doing laundry. The bread uses biga as a dough starter, and it has to sit overnight before you make the bread. Like most breads, focaccia doesn't require much hands-on time, but you will need to work with it periodically over the course of a day.

The biga can be made up to three days before you want to bake. You can also use sourdough starter if you have it. Biga will decrease in volume if you try to measure it in cups; therefore, it's best to use a kitchen scale for this recipe.

—*Benjamin Smart* BIG GROVE BREWERY | SOLON, IA

BIGA
250 grams warm water (80°F)
250 grams bread flour
2 grams yeast

MUSHROOMS
2 tablespoons olive oil
1 pound mushrooms, oyster, maitake, or shiitake (your favorite kind will do)
½ cup sliced shallots
½ teaspoon kosher salt, or to taste
1 tablespoon minced fresh summer savory or thyme

FOCACCIA
700 grams warm water (80°F)
150 grams Biga or sourdough starter
50 grams olive oil, plus more for coating
1 kilogram bread flour
25 grams kosher salt
5 grams yeast
Sea salt, for sprinkling

WHERE TO FIND...

Mushrooms
Anything But Green Gardens
Vinton, IA

TO MAKE THE BIGA

In a large bowl, mix the ingredients together to form a dough. Cover the bowl with plastic wrap and leave at room temperature for 1½ hours to ferment, then place in the refrigerator overnight.

The next day, set the bowl on the countertop to bring the dough back to room temperature, and start on the mushrooms.

TO MAKE THE MUSHROOMS

In a medium sauté pan, heat the olive oil over medium heat. Once the oil shimmers, add the mushrooms and sauté until they are slightly browned and softened. Add the shallots and continue cooking until the shallots are translucent and most of the moisture has been cooked out of the mushrooms. Add the salt and season to taste. Fold in the savory. Set aside.

TO MAKE THE FOCACCIA

In a large bowl, place the water, 150 grams of biga, and the olive oil and whisk to combine. Don't worry if the mixture doesn't completely come together. Add the flour, salt, and yeast and stir with a wooden spoon until the flour is hydrated and you have a sticky, bumpy, homogeneous dough. Cover with plastic wrap. After 30 minutes, add the mushrooms. Wet your hands, then lift and fold the dough over onto itself 3 times. Re-cover with plastic wrap. Continue this series of folding the dough every 30 minutes for 3 hours.

Generously coat the bottom of 2 large, rimmed baking sheets with the olive oil. Divide the dough in half and place 1 half on each sheet. Pour more olive oil on top of each half of the dough, coating it completely to keep it from drying out. Cover with plastic wrap. Over the next 1 to 1½ hours, gently stretch and dimple the dough with your fingers, ultimately stretching the dough almost to the edges of the baking sheets.

Preheat the oven to 450°F.

Bake the focaccia for 8 minutes, rotate the baking sheets, and bake for 6 to 10 more minutes, until the focaccia is a nice dark golden brown. Remove the focaccia from the oven, drizzle with a little more of the olive oil, and sprinkle a light layer of sea salt over the top.

Note: This focaccia made without the mushrooms is excellent for the Open-Faced Caponata and Heirloom Tomato Sandwich (p. 77).

Stuffed Squash Blossoms

SERVES 6

This fast and simple recipe is a wonderful way to use up squash blossoms. The basic filling can be amended with an herb of your choice, and the final product can be enjoyed alone or dressed with shaved prosciutto. Espelette pepper provides a subtle complex heat similar to a blend of paprika and cayenne pepper. You can find it online and in specialty spice shops.

—Paul Kulik   THE BOILER ROOM | OMAHA, NE

2 medium Yukon gold potatoes

1 cup ricotta (homemade preferred, see p. 89 or 97)

12–15 squash blossoms

Scant ½ cup prosecco

¼ cup cornstarch

1 teaspoon baking soda

¾ teaspoon salt, plus more to taste

½ teaspoon ground Espelette pepper, plus more to taste

2 cups sunflower oil

Shaved prosciutto, for garnish (optional)

WHERE TO FIND...

Squash Blossoms
Squeaky Green Organics
Omaha, NE

Potatoes
Blooms Organic
Crescent, IA

Preheat the oven to 400°F.

Wrap the potatoes in aluminum foil and roast in the oven until soft, about 45 minutes to 1 hour. Slice the potatoes in half, scoop out the flesh, and pass the flesh through a potato ricer. You will need 1 cup of riced potatoes.

In a large bowl, combine the riced potatoes with the ricotta. Fill a pastry bag with the mixture. A plastic zip-top bag with the corner cut off would also work.

Gently open each squash blossom and pinch out the stamen and pistils. Holding the blossom in one hand and the pastry bag in the other, pipe about 1 teaspoon of the filling into the blossom. Lightly press the petals together and twist the tops, just a bit.

In a large bowl, whisk together the prosecco, cornstarch, baking soda, salt, and Espelette pepper. You may not need all the prosecco. Add more cornstarch if necessary to thicken the batter to your desired consistency. Keep in mind, however, that it should be fairly lightweight.

In a large, deep sauté pan, heat the sunflower oil to 360°F. Coat each stuffed blossom in the batter and deep fry for about 90 seconds, or until golden brown. Place on a rack to drain any excess oil and season to taste with a little salt and Espelette. Garnish with the shaved prosciutto if desired.

Note: If needed, you can use a clipping of chive to gently tie the blossom petals together before frying. Just cut it off before serving.

Kevin Shinn

CHEF BREAD AND CUP | 440 N. 8TH ST., SUITE 150 | LINCOLN, NE |
402.438.2255 | BREADANDCUP.COM

Upon entering Bread and Cup in Lincoln, guests walk down a long hallway flanked by stacks of flour bags, wine bottles, and windows on one side, with the kitchen and bakery on the other side. The walkway leads to a relaxed dining room blanketed in neutral colors and minimal but meaningful mementos. Two large doors with crackling alligator paint are suspended from the west wall. A tin flower bucket brimming with Bells of Ireland, towering blue delphinium, and snapdragons in white and violet adorn the aged entryways salvaged from the home of Kevin Shinn's grandmother.

"Some of my most vivid food memories revolved around my maternal grandmother," says Kevin, who, along with his wife, Karen, opened the restaurant in 2007. "I was probably seven at the time. We went to her neighbor's house, sat on the front porch, and snapped beans all afternoon in the hot, hot Oklahoma sun, but something about it was extremely endearing. My grandmother sitting there, gossiping with the neighbors . . . it was idyllic, I think, now, because I want it to be."

Although the memory was of an isolated childhood experience, the significance of how food brings people together left a lasting impression on Kevin, who sees food as a vehicle to build and enhance relationships.

"Food is a horribly, horribly intimate act," he says. "I am making you something that you are going to put into your body. You're trusting me to consume this. That it's going to taste good. That it won't be bad for you. At the same time, I'm worried about your response to my gift. I want your approval. I want to know that I've delighted you. That exchange is risky. It's horribly risky."

The intimacy involved in feeding others is primarily why Kevin uses local producers. They have a common understanding in the work each is trying to elevate and the outcomes they both want to achieve—good food and strong relationships. Buying from a farmer he knows and trusts to provide the quality he expects is paramount to achieving an inviting and rewarding experience for those who visit Bread and Cup. When the ingredients are exceptional, preparation can be simple and diners can enjoy each other, while the food serves as a pleasantry in the background of their day—an essential component for Kevin. ■

Squash Swirl Soup

SERVES 6 (2 CUPS PER PERSON)

Some vegetables are bold and sanguine, like beets and celery, but others are much more subtle and phlegmatic in making their presence known. Squash fits into that latter category. It's why cooks end up putting zucchini in muffin recipes—they can hide it easily. This recipe allows you to appreciate the nuances of both acorn squash and butternut squash side by side in the same bowl. Both colors create a visually appealing presentation.

—Kevin Shinn BREAD AND CUP | LINCOLN, NE

2 acorn squash

2 butternut squash

2 onions, finely diced

4 cloves garlic, minced

8 cups water, divided

2 tablespoons butter, divided

2 tablespoons heavy cream, divided

½ teaspoon salt, divided, or to taste

WHERE TO FIND...

Squash
Sanders Specialty Meats and Produce
Dwight, NE

Preheat the oven to 325°F.

With a sturdy knife, carefully split each squash in half. Scoop out the seeds using a spoon. If you have a grapefruit spoon, that works great for scooping out squash seeds. Place the squash on a baking sheet cut side down and bake until tender, at least 1 hour.

While the squash is baking, in a medium sauté pan, sweat the onions and garlic over medium-low heat. Sweating is the process in which low, gentle heat draws out the moisture, causing the outer appearance of the onion to look shiny and wet. This helps enhance the flavor of the onion. I tell my cooks to make the onions sweat, not cry. If you can hear the onions sizzle, the heat is too high. After about 10 to 15 minutes of sweating, divide the onions and garlic evenly into 2 stockpots or saucepans.

When the squash is tender, remove from the oven and let cool before handling. A gentle spray of cold water can speed the cooling process. Scoop out the squash, keeping the acorn and butternut squash separate. Place the acorn squash into one pot and the butternut squash into the other. To start, add 2 cups of the water to each and bring to a simmer.

With an immersion blender, purée each soup. A blender or food processor can also be used to purée the soup, but extra care is needed in transferring the hot liquids. At this point, add more water ¼ cup at a time to each pot until you reach your desired viscosity (you may not use all the water). Both purées should have the same consistency: thin enough so that your spoon doesn't stand straight up, but thick enough to be velvety. Add 1 tablespoon of the butter and 1 tablespoon of the cream to each soup for smoothness and flavor. Season to taste with the salt.

Using two ladles, one for each soup, ladle the soups side by side into the same bowl. Serve. The acorn squash has a sweeter flavor and a lighter yellow color, while the butternut is darker orange and less sweet. Your guests can taste each soup separately or swirl them together to combine the squash flavors.

Spicy Brussels Sprouts

SERVES 8

Brussels sprouts are at their absolute best when the weather still has a chill. The blend of end-of-season tomatoes and best-of-season sprouts makes a great weeknight side.

—*Sean Wilson* PROOF | DES MOINES, IA

1 teaspoon coriander seeds

1 teaspoon cumin seeds

1 teaspoon caraway seeds

1½ cups diced bacon

6 cups halved brussels sprouts

½ teaspoon ground turmeric

3–5 jalapeño chilies, membranes and seeds removed, minced

1 tablespoon butter

5 Roma tomatoes, chopped and deseeded (about 1½ cups)

Salt and freshly ground pepper, to taste

WHERE TO FIND...

Brussels Sprouts
TableTop Farm
Nevada, IA

Tomatoes
Butcher Crick Farms
Carlisle, IA

In a large sauté pan over medium heat, toast the coriander, cumin, and caraway seeds. This should take about 45 seconds to 1 minute. Remove the spices from the pan and set aside.

In the same pan, cook the bacon over medium heat until it's crisp. Using a slotted spoon, remove the bacon and set aside. Leave the bacon fat in the pan.

Add the brussels sprouts, toasted spices, and turmeric to the pan. Stir to coat. Cover and cook over medium–low heat for about 20 to 25 minutes, until the sprouts get a little color on them but are still crisp-tender. Stir in the minced jalapeños and butter. Add the tomatoes and cook for about 10 more minutes. Remove from the heat and stir in the bacon. Season to taste with the salt and pepper. Serve.

Terra and Matthew Hall

FARMERS RHIZOSPHERE FARM | MISSOURI VALLEY, IA |
RHIZOSPHEREFARM.ORG

M atthew Hall leans forward with his elbows on his knees. His head is down. He is playing with the silver wedding band that glows against his sun-stained skin. Nearly two months before today's conversation, he was working in the fields with his back bent toward the sky and his fingers knuckle-deep in the soil of a sweet potato bed. His wife, Terra, had just loaded up the truck and driven across the Missouri River to make their first deliveries of the season to CSA members. Then the skies changed color.

They founded Rhizosphere Farm in 2009, on the Nebraska side of the river, and spent the next three years cultivating rented land. Eventually the couple decided to take a chance and invest in land of their own. The stakes were high; such a decision meant they would have to take a year

off of farming, suspend their restaurant client relationships, and live with Matthew's parents while they worked multiple jobs and saved money. Even still, it was a risk they were willing to take. To be a farmer, you have to be gambler, and Matthew and Terra committed to rolling the dice.

"This was the last place we looked at. We pulled up at about six p.m. one night and I said, 'This is it.' We hadn't seen anything but the field," Matthew says. They put every penny they had and whatever else they could scrounge together for the down payment on a six-acre farm with four outbuildings and a little log cabin in Missouri Valley.

Matthew's voice is deep and his words are chosen slowly, like a man who still doubts what his eyes told him. He and one of his field hands knew the storm was imminent and took shelter in the log cabin moments before the June sky broke open. In some ways, the storm was commonplace. It was just another in a series of tumultuous weather events to come through the area, but while the other storms were damaging, this one was devastating. Only 10 minutes later, Matthew and the field hand emerged from the cabin to see the fields turned to mush and the first half of their farming season annihilated by hail the size of golf balls.

To be a farmer, you have to be gambler, and Matthew and Terra committed to rolling the dice.

Less than two months has passed since that afternoon. Matthew sits under the low roofline of the cabin and raises his head, but his body remains hunched forward. His eyes scan the rows of vegetables replanted for the third time this season with a sense of frustration, hope, and exhaustion. It's July and they have made $210.

"Did I cry when the storms came?" he asks. "No, but I've cried a lot since then."

A rooster crows, and in the distance, a train blows its whistle, subtle reminders of what built this quiet community. The sun is setting now; the gauzelike clouds that linger motionless in the sky filter its orange glow. Terra looks at Matthew in the way that only a wife can, sharing in his heartache as they work together to put the pieces of this life back in place. When a storm comes in the fall, at least farmers have harvested and sold something. The plants are established and those in the ground—like potatoes—are protected by the soil that covers them. That's not the case in the spring. In the spring, endless blue skies set against freshly worked soil are a deceptive dealer; the winds come quickly and the storms are fierce. A spring storm can take everything, including a farmer's livelihood, but even more damaging is the blow it deals to a farmer's grit.

Rhizosphere Farm is known for providing impeccable vegetables packaged so beautifully it feels like Christmas every time a box is opened. Food grown with such expertise not only inspires creativity but also acts as a cornerstone for the cultural foundation of a community—without the farmer, there is no weekend trip to farmers' markets, no weekly deliveries to consumers, no wholesale deliveries to chefs. Dining and shopping experiences are forever changed.

The Grey Plume and The French Bulldog, two restaurants in Omaha, Nebraska, that benefit from Matthew and Terra's skill in the fields, volunteered their time and resources to host a 175-person farm-to-table dinner. The intention was to raise money for Rhizosphere Farm so the Halls could invest in fall plantings. What the chefs hoped would serve as a housewarming gift for two of their favorite farmers became a lifeline after the storm.

"I think in many ways, that dinner was a turning point for us. The support was encouraging, of course, but after a while you just feel like everything is coming for you," says Terra, who explains that more storms were predicted the day of the field dinner. "Everybody was watching the weather on their phones; we had a few light sprinkles and then we all watched that storm roll right by."

Terra's love for agriculture grew slowly from her experience as a Peace Corps volunteer in Mali. It was there she realized that a community could feed itself without the use of chemicals and survive. Her desire to effect social change continued when she worked as a community activist in Oregon. From there, she assumed the role that put all the pieces of her life together from both a career and personal perspective: an apprenticeship at Horton Road Organics, a farm 45 minutes outside Eugene, Oregon. It's where she met Matthew, and together they gained a hands-on education in delivery mechanisms and greenhouse and field management. It wasn't long after working at Horton that Terra realized her social ideals could come to fruition through farming.

"You put these seeds in the ground, and it's all hope. Hope and hard work," a fellow farmer once told Matthew. "The seeds are growing and the tomatoes look great, or they have a disease and it's over. Even the best of the best have to have a flair for dramatic enterprise. You just gotta be kind of nuts to do it; you gotta be a gambler." ■

Pork–Fennel Sausage with Pickled Mustard Seeds

SERVES 6

I developed this sausage for a fall restaurant menu. The use of fresh fennel and citrus zest distinguishes this sausage and provides the clean and bright aspects we desired.

Most pork shoulders have an ideal 25 percent to 30 percent fat content, which is required for flavor as well as to keep the sausage from drying out. Once stuffed, it's important to rest the sausage in the refrigerator overnight to help secure the link twists. If this is your first time making sausage from scratch, you may want to work with a friend, as an extra set of hands can be helpful. If you are comfortable with making sausage, feel free to double or triple the recipe.

The pickled mustard seeds are a nice condiment and provide a bit of simple texture. They require one month to soften in the vinegar, so plan ahead.

—Bryce Coulton THE FRENCH BULLDOG | OMAHA, NE

PICKLED MUSTARD SEEDS

1 cup whole yellow and/or black mustard seeds

1–1½ cups vinegar (apple cider, white wine, or champagne)

PORK-FENNEL SAUSAGE

6 feet 32- or 35-mm diameter hog casings, obtained from your butcher

2 pounds boneless pork shoulder, ground (70:30 ratio of lean meat to fat)

5 ounces finely chopped fresh fennel bulb (about 1 cup)

3 teaspoons kosher salt

2½ teaspoons ground white pepper

1½ teaspoons freshly ground black pepper

1½ teaspoons finely chopped garlic (about 2–3 large cloves)

1½ teaspoons ground fennel seeds

½ teaspoon finely chopped fresh rosemary

1 fresh bay leaf, finely chopped

Zest of 1 orange

Zest of ½ lemon

Zest of ½ lime

TO MAKE THE PICKLED MUSTARD SEEDS

In a sealable container, place the mustard seeds. Pour the vinegar over the seeds, making sure all seeds are submerged. Cover and store in the refrigerator. Over time, the seeds will absorb the vinegar. You will need to top off the vinegar approximately every 10 days to keep the seeds covered.

After 30 days, drain the seeds and discard the vinegar. A fine-mesh strainer works great for this. To prevent a bitter taste, return the seeds to the container for another 3 days before use. They will keep for an additional 30 days.

TO MAKE THE SAUSAGE

Hog casings are usually stored in a brine or salt pack. To prepare the hog casings, rinse them: find one of the open ends and run water through the casing, making sure to loosen any knots or twists that might have formed. Soak the casings in warm water for 1 hour prior to use.

Next, set up your meat grinder and sausage stuffer. It's impossible to describe exact instructions because there are so many grinders available on the market, so follow the instructions of your grinder. Never use your hand to push meat into the feed tube. If your stuffer attachment sits high, it's helpful to have a tray to catch the links as you twist them. A baking sheet on top of a large bowl placed beneath the stuffer attachment works well for this.

Separate the pork shoulder into pieces small enough to fit into the feed tube of your grinder. Place in the refrigerator while you prepare the other ingredients.

In a large bowl, combine all of the other sausage ingredients. Set the bowl nearby.

Continued

Grind the meat and add it to the bowl. Using your hands, combine the spices and meat, working the mixture until a handful can stick to your palm for a few seconds. This ensures the sausage will hold together and not fall apart. Place the bowl in the refrigerator. If you want to test the seasoning, take a small bit of meat, form it into a patty, and fry it up. Taste, then adjust the seasoning to the rest of the meat as needed.

Slide the hog casings onto the stuffer tube, being careful not to twist the casing, and tie it off at the end. If you have trouble sliding the casing onto the stuffer tube, run water through the casing as you are sliding it onto the tube. Use a toothpick or a skewer to poke a small hole in the casing once it's been tied off, to release air.

Attach the stuffer tube and load the meat into the sausage stuffer platform. Send the meat through and begin to stuff the casings. You want your sausage firm, but not hard. It should yield to pressure but not be squishy. Create a link by measuring 5 inches from an end, pinching the link, and rotating the link away from you. Continue to create links by measuring another 5 inches, pinching the link, and twisting it away from you. Once you've finished twisting your links, tie off the last one. Remove any air pockets by pricking the links a few times with a skewer or toothpick. Place the links on a baking sheet, transfer to the refrigerator, and allow them to sit overnight, which helps secure the twists.

To cook, you can grill the sausage or heat it in a sauté pan on the stove. Make sure the internal temperature reaches 145°F. Cut the sausage on the bias and serve with 1 or 2 spoonfuls of pickled mustard seeds.

Notes: You may notice some meat remains in the grinder. To get it out, send some bread through the grinder. Use the bread-sausage mixture to form some patties. Cook them on medium heat in a sauté pan and enjoy.

Stored in the refrigerator, the sausage should be used within 3 days. You can package and store it in the freezer for up to 3 months.

WHERE TO FIND...

Pork
Truebridge Foods
Omaha, NE

Herbs, Fennel
Rhizosphere Farm
Missouri Valley, IA

George and Emily Johnson

ARTISANS GEORGE PAUL VINEGAR | CODY, NE | WWW.GEORGEPAULVINEGAR.COM

George Johnson folded up an article he had clipped out of last month's *Omaha World-Herald* and put it in his pocket. After pulling on his muck boots and Carhartt jacket, he gently placed one slender, perfectly labeled vinegar bottle after another into a cardboard box. He then drove 340 miles from his home in Cody, through the undulating and snow-covered Sandhills, to Omaha.

Once the country roads turned to interstates, then city streets, and finally into the red cobblestones of Omaha's historic Old Market district, he took the newspaper clipping from his pocket and set out to find the first top chef on its list. One by one, he dropped in on them, unannounced and unknown, to offer a sample of the small-batch artisanal vinegars he made from grapes grown in the Sandhills.

The chefs fell in love with his craftsmanship, and many remain customers to this day. Their adoration marked the first true validation he had received after years of work, risk, and determination to create the slightly acidic, fruit-forward elixirs that bear his name.

George started his vinegar career as a hobby winemaker. Foraging for wild grapes with his daughter, Emily, during her visits home from Reed College in Portland, Oregon, became a way for the two to spend time together. As the years passed and college classes gave way to professional opportunities, their casual conversations became more like business meetings, where father and daughter discussed the real-world market for Nebraska wines.

"We got to the point where we could make really good wine, but it's never going to taste like a cab or a pinot," said Emily from her home in Oregon, where she lives for part of the year and operates her letterpress business, Emprint. "It's never going to have the same qualities that people expect from wine. People would buy it because it was novel. We wanted to know how to scale it up to where we could sell it in California."

During one of Emily's visits home she brought her friend Noah with her. They sat around the dinner table with George and Karen, George's wife of 40 years, talking, philosophizing, and discussing the potential appeal of the wine they were enjoying, when Noah suggested they make vinegar.

"He kept saying that he thought it would make great vinegar, which is kind of an insult to a winemaker, although he didn't mean it that way," Emily said with a laugh. "He mentioned it so many times, we started looking into the idea."

Eventually, George applied for a grant to conduct market research and discovered that vinegar had huge potential. The Johnson family decided it was time to take a leap of faith and transform their wine-making project into a vinegar business based in their hometown of 160 people. George and Karen cleared space in their large backyard and constructed an environmentally friendly and energy-efficient vinegary.

"Being environmentally responsible is very important, even for a small business," said Emily. "Old world is not just about creating a product, but about a company philosophy and its approach to business. Our building needed to be warm, comforting, and homey."

They finished the building, made from straw bales and covered in stucco, in 2009. A few months later, George took that fateful trip to Omaha, where he poured samples of Temparia, a single-varietal, floral vinegar, into whiskey glasses and asked the chefs to have a taste. Looking back, George says he is proud of the work, but that after years of false starts, some wins, and some losses, his business success means nothing compared to the friends he's made along the way, the longevity of his marriage to Karen, and the love of his children. ■

Bobwhite Quail with Butternut Squash and Honey–Butter Apples

SERVES 4

Dave and Lori Sanders own Sanders Specialty Meats and Produce, just east of Lincoln, Nebraska. They raise quail, rabbits, and bees; they also cure a wide variety of local meats for area chefs. The bobwhite quail in this recipe is indigenous to Nebraska and is a perfect fit for fall.

Small's Fruit Farm is in Mondamin, Iowa, overlooking the Missouri River Valley. Jim Small and his family have been growing fruit on this land for decades and specialize in apples. We did not use a specific type of apple for this recipe, because we felt any local apple this time of year would work.

Shadow Brook Farm, just east of Lincoln, is a breath of fresh air for us during the late fall and winter months, as produce becomes scarce.

George Johnson of George Paul Vinegar is a true artisan who creates a product unlike anything else available on the market today.

This recipe requires 24 hours for the quail to marinate, so keep that in mind when planning your menu. The quantity is easily adjustable for more or fewer guests.

—*Clayton Chapman* THE GREY PLUME | OMAHA, NE

BUTTERNUT SQUASH

1 butternut squash, peeled, seeded, and cut into ¼-inch slices

1 teaspoon finely ground high-quality coffee beans

1 teaspoon ground cinnamon

Kosher salt and freshly ground black pepper, to taste

3 sprigs fresh thyme

4 tablespoons unsalted butter

2 tablespoons dark honey

Place the quail in a nonreactive container and pour the brewed coffee over them. Make sure the quail are completely covered and there is space between them. Marinate in the refrigerator for a minimum of 1 hour, up to 24 hours. Once the quail have marinated, removed them from the coffee, pat dry, and set aside. Reserve 2 cups of the coffee.

Preheat the oven to 350°F.

Create an aluminum foil package large enough to hold the squash. Place the sliced squash into the foil package and season with the ground coffee, cinnamon, salt, and pepper. Top with the thyme sprigs and dot with the butter. Wrap the foil around the squash so it is completely covered; the goal is to have very tender squash without any browning. Place the squash package onto one side of a large baking sheet, leaving the other side available for the quail, which you will add later. Place the baking sheet in the oven. Bake for about 20 to 25 minutes.

Season the quail on all sides with the ground coffee, salt, and pepper.

In a medium pan, heat the oil over medium–high heat. Once the oil is hot, add the quail to the pan and sear on all sides. Set the quail aside and begin the coffee sauce.

QUAIL AND COFFEE SAUCE

4 whole bobwhite quail

4 cups high-quality brewed coffee (can still be warm)

1 tablespoon finely ground high-quality coffee beans

Kosher salt and freshly ground black pepper, to taste

3 tablespoons oil

8 sprigs fresh thyme, divided

1 tablespoon dark honey

1 tablespoon George Paul red wine vinegar

1 tablespoon unsalted butter

Zest of 1 lemon, for garnish

HONEY-BUTTER APPLES

3 tablespoons unsalted butter

2 apples (skin on), cored and cut into ¼-inch slices

2 tablespoons dark honey

2 tablespoons George Paul white wine vinegar

Kosher salt and freshly ground black pepper, to taste

1½ teaspoons minced fresh parsley, for garnish

Gently wipe out the oil from the pan you seared the quail in. Add the reserved coffee to the pan. Be careful, as the liquid could splatter. Add 4 of the thyme sprigs. Bring the mixture to a simmer and reduce the sauce to ¼ cup, stirring occasionally.

Once the sauce has reduced for about 10 minutes, and the squash has been in the oven for about 20 to 25 minutes, add the seared quail to the baking sheet with the squash. Top with the remaining thyme sprigs, 1 for each quail, and bake until the internal temperature of the thigh reaches 160°F, about 20 to 25 minutes.

While the coffee sauce is continuing to reduce, and the quail and squash are still in the oven, start your honey–butter apples. In a sauté pan, heat the butter over medium–high heat. Once the butter foams, add the apples and cook until crisp on the outside and tender on the inside, about 4 minutes. Add the honey and white wine vinegar. Season to taste with the salt and pepper. Keep warm over low heat until ready to serve.

At this stage, the coffee sauce should be thick and reduced. Remove and discard the thyme sprigs. Whisk in the honey and red wine vinegar. Finish the sauce by stirring in the butter and seasoning to taste with the salt and pepper.

Once the quail thighs have reached 160°F, remove the pan from the oven, remove and discard the thyme sprigs, and brush the quail with the coffee sauce. Set aside.

Empty the squash into a medium bowl, add the honey, and season to taste with the salt and pepper. Stir, then mash with a potato masher for a more rustic appearance. You could also purée the mixture if you want a smoother consistency.

Divide the squash evenly among 4 plates. Spoon the apples on top of the squash, then sprinkle with the minced parsley. Place 1 quail on top of the apples. Sprinkle with the lemon zest and serve.

WHERE TO FIND...

Bobwhite Quail, Honey	Apples	Butternut Squash	Vinegar
Sanders Specialty Meats and Produce Dwight, NE	Small's Fruit Farm Mondamin, IA	Shadow Brook Farm Lincoln, NE	George Paul Vinegar Cody, NE

Renee and Jim Small

FARMERS SMALL'S FRUIT FARM | MONDAMIN, IA | SMALLSFRUITFARM.COM

For most of us, the first warm spring days bring welcome relief from winter, but Renee and Jim Small look at the ebb and flow of temperatures differently. The promise of fruit from all of those early blossoms can end with one solid frost. Their hoarse and hearty laughter is often bookmarked by sleepless nights and fears of crop loss.

"There's a lot of seriousness on a farm. A lot of it. So you have to laugh when things are going all right," says Renee. "While everyone is talking about how great the weather is in early spring, we are hoping we don't lose everything in a coming frost. We don't say it, but that's what we're thinking."

Fruit farmers can't replant a crop of apple trees in a season. If an early heat wave causes the trees to bloom before the threat of frost is completely over, the Smalls lose their entire income for the year. With concerns such as these, it's easy to wonder why anyone would run an orchard. Although Renee can't say why others do it, she knows why she and Jim do.

"I've seen people come in with their children and then their grandchildren. We get to see generation after generation bring their families out and enjoy the farm and have a great day."

Jim is a fifth-generation fruit farmer, and, like many generational farmers, he doesn't romanticize the job. "It's really the only thing I've ever done," he adds.

In 1894, his great-great grandfather bought some apples from a farmer in the Loess Hills. He thought they were the best apples he had ever had, so the following year he returned to buy the orchard and started what became the family business. Jim's son, Trevor, and Trevor's wife, Stacy, have shown some interest in the farm, and he hopes it will continue to live on in the family for at least one more generation—but he also knows an orchard is a big commitment.

"It's always busy. There's always something to do on a farm," says Jim. The branches he pruned from more than 30 varieties of apple, apricot, and cherry trees during the winter months were used to start warming fires in April. It saved some of the harvest, but there weren't many apricots this year; the late frost just didn't spare them. ■

"We get to see generation after generation bring their families out and enjoy the farm and have a great day."

Pappardelle with Spicy Heirloom Tomato Sauce

SERVES 6

Although tomatoes are often thought of as a summer fruit, it's not uncommon in Nebraska to pick them from your garden as late as October. The wide pappardelle is the perfect vehicle for carrying this rustic, spicy tomato sauce straight into your mouth. The pasta dough can be made months ahead of time and frozen, either as nests of noodles or as dough slabs waiting to be rolled out. Fresh pasta dough will turn green if left in the refrigerator for more than one day; once it's done resting, use it or freeze it. You could also make the tomato sauce ahead of time, as it freezes beautifully.

—*Nick Strawhecker* DANTE RISTORANTE PIZZERIA | OMAHA, NE

TOMATO SAUCE

3 pounds heirloom tomatoes, mixed varieties

2 tablespoons olive oil

1 medium onion, chopped (about 1 cup)

5 cloves garlic, chopped

½ teaspoon salt, or to taste

½ teaspoons freshly ground black pepper, or to taste

PAPPARDELLE

1½ cups all-purpose flour, plus more as needed

14 egg yolks

1½ teaspoons olive oil

½ teaspoon salt

FINISHED SAUCE

½ pound pancetta, diced

2 tablespoons minced shallots (about 1 shallot)

2 cloves garlic, sliced

1 teaspoon red pepper flakes

¾ cup white wine

Tomato Sauce

½ cup torn fresh basil

2 tablespoons olive oil, plus more to taste

Salt and freshly ground black pepper, to taste

TO MAKE THE TOMATO SAUCE

Bring a large pot of water to a boil. Score an *X* through the skin on the bottom of each tomato. Place the tomatoes into the boiling water for about 10 to 15 seconds. Using a slotted spoon, remove the tomatoes from the pot. Peel and core, removing and discarding the skin and core. Roughly chop the tomatoes, then set aside.

In a large saucepan, heat the oil over medium–low heat. Add the onion and sweat it for 20 to 25 minutes. You want the onion to soften, without browning. Add the garlic and sauté until fragrant, about 1 minute. Add the tomatoes and simmer for about 1½ hours, until the tomatoes are falling apart, most of the moisture has evaporated, and the sauce is thick. Once finished, remove from the heat but leave on the stove. Season to taste with salt and pepper.

While the sauce cooks, make the pappardelle.

TO MAKE THE PAPPARDELLE

Depending on your level of comfort, pasta dough can be made on the countertop or in a large mixing bowl. Create a mountain of the flour and then push down in the middle to form a well. Place the egg yolks, olive oil, and salt into the well. Using a fork, slowly whisk the yolks, pulling in bits of the flour as you go. Working from the inside of the well out, gradually combine the wet and dry ingredients until the dough has somewhat come together. Transfer to a clean surface and knead for about 10 minutes. The dough should be smooth, elastic, and not sticky. If it's sticky, knead in more flour, 1 teaspoon at a time, until it reaches the proper consistency. Wrap the dough with plastic wrap or a clean towel and let rest in the refrigerator for 1 hour.

Continued

WHERE TO FIND...

Tomatoes, Onion
Rhizosphere Farm
Missouri Valley, IA

Pancetta
La Quercia
Norwalk, IA

Remove the dough from the refrigerator and cut it into quarters. On a well-floured surface, roll out the dough until it's not quite paper thin. Once the dough has reached your desired thinness, dust the top with flour and then gently fold it over on itself into a stack. Cut the stack into 1-inch-wide strips. If using the same day, keep a slightly damp towel on the pappardelle so it doesn't dry out. If saving for later, create little nests of noodles on a well-floured baking sheet, then place in the freezer. Once frozen, transfer the nests to a plastic bag.

TO FINISH THE SAUCE AND ASSEMBLE THE DISH

In a large sauté pan over medium–low heat, cook the pancetta for about 30 minutes. Keep about 40 percent of the rendered fat and discard or save the rest for another day. Add the shallots, garlic, and red pepper flakes to the pan. Sauté for about 1 minute, being careful not to burn the garlic. Add the white wine and scrape up any brown bits from the bottom of the pan. Cook until the wine is reduced by ½. Add all of the prepared tomato sauce. Turn up the heat and bring the mixture to a boil, then reduce the heat and let simmer for 20 to 30 minutes, until much of the moisture evaporates and you are left with a thick, hearty sauce. Keep warm.

Bring a large pot of salted water to a boil. Add the pappardelle and cook for 1 to 2 minutes. Reserve about 1 cup of the pasta water, then drain the pappardelle.

Add the pappardelle to the sauce. Add the basil and olive oil and heat, constantly stirring, for 2 to 3 minutes. If it starts to dry out, add the reserved pasta water, 1 tablespoon at a time. Season to taste with the salt and pepper. Serve.

Butternut Squash Ravioli with Brown Butter and Apples

SERVES 6 (ABOUT 38 RAVIOLI)

I grew up in a house where gardening and cooking were a big part of daily life. My mother always made homemade pasta, and my father spent many hours in the garden. This recipe is a tribute to them.

—*George Formaro* CENTRO | DES MOINES, IA

PASTA DOUGH

2–2¼ cups all-purpose flour

4 eggs

2 teaspoons olive oil

⅛ teaspoon salt

FILLING

1 2-pound butternut squash

½ cup ricotta cheese

½ cup grated Prairie Breeze cheese or mild white cheddar cheese

½ cup grated Prairie Rose cheese or swiss cheese

1 tablespoon ground parmesan cheese

1 teaspoon ground ginger

1 teaspoon salt, or to taste

½ teaspoon freshly ground black pepper, or to taste

¼ teaspoon freshly ground nutmeg

SAUCE

½ cup (1 stick) unsalted butter

1–2 red-skinned apples, cored and cut into ¼-inch pieces

2 teaspoons chopped garlic (about 3 cloves)

15 fresh sage leaves

Salt and freshly ground black pepper, to taste

Grated parmesan cheese, for garnish

Scoop 2 cups of the flour onto a large cutting board or countertop. Create a well in the flour with a wide hole in the center. (This should resemble a volcano.) Place the eggs, olive oil, and salt into the well. Put your hand inside the well and make a stirring motion, pulling in flour from the inside and working your way out. Knead until a soft dough forms and no longer sticks to your fingers. The dough should feel elastic, but not sticky. If it's sticky, add a little more flour, 1 tablespoon at a time. Wrap the dough in plastic wrap and let rest in the refrigerator for 30 minutes to 1 hour.

Preheat the oven to 375°F.

Halve the butternut squash and scoop out the seeds. Place the squash skin side down on a baking sheet and bake for 45 minutes to 1 hour, or until the flesh can easily be pierced with a fork.

When cool enough to handle, scoop out 2 cups' worth of the flesh from the shell and place in a medium bowl. Using a potato masher or a fork, mash the squash. Add the cheeses, ginger, salt, pepper, and nutmeg and stir to combine. Set aside to cool.

Remove the pasta dough from the refrigerator. Using a knife or pastry blade, cut the dough into quarters. Rewrap the pieces you aren't using and set aside. Fill a small bowl with a little bit of water and set it next to your work area.

You can use a stand mixer with a pasta-roller attachment or roll out the pasta by hand with a rolling pin. I prefer to roll it out by hand because of the rustic look it gives the pasta. On a well-floured surface, roll out your dough into a long, thin strip about 6 inches wide. Roll it as thin as you can, less than ⅛ inch. Keep moving the dough around on your work surface so it doesn't stick. You can do this by pulling one end of the dough over your rolling pin, then using the pin to lift the dough off your work surface. Once the dough is thin enough, place 1 tablespoon of the squash mixture, about every 2 fingers' width apart, along the length of the dough.

Continued

Dip your fingers in the bowl of water and then run them around the filling mounds. Fold the dough over the filling. Work from the mounds out to gently press the top layer of dough to the bottom layer. Try not to trap air into the pockets. Cut between the mounds with a knife. Press the edges together with your fingers, or use a fork to seal the ravioli. You want to have about a ½-inch pasta border around each mound of filling. Place the finished ravioli on a floured baking sheet. Be careful not to let the ravioli touch each other.

Repeat these steps with the remaining dough until the dough is used up. Transfer the baking sheet of ravioli to the freezer, or cover with plastic wrap and let the ravioli rest for 1 hour before cooking. The resting helps the seals set, so the ravioli will be less likely to open when boiled.

In a medium sauté pan over low heat, begin to brown the butter. As it melts, swirl the butter occasionally. It will turn yellow and foamy, then light brown, and finally medium brown with a nutty aroma. This will take about 15 minutes. Butter can go from browned to burned very quickly, so keep an eye on it.

Meanwhile, bring a large pot of salted water to a boil. Add the ravioli. If fresh, the ravioli will take 4 to 5 minutes to cook; if frozen, they will take about 8 minutes.

Add the apple and garlic to the pan with the brown butter and cook for about 2 to 3 more minutes. Add the sage leaves and cook for 1 to 2 more minutes. Season to taste with the salt and pepper. Remove the pan from the heat.

Drain the ravioli and transfer to a large bowl. Pour the brown-butter sauce over the ravioli, then toss gently to coat. Garnish with the grated parmesan cheese and serve.

WHERE TO FIND...

Butternut Squash
Cleverley Farms
Mingo, IA

Prairie Breeze and
Prairie Rose Cheeses
Milton Creamery
Milton, IA

Larry Cleverley

FARMER CLEVERLEY FARMS | MINGO, IA |
WWW.FACEBOOK.COM/CLEVERLEYFARMS

East of Highway 330 North in Mingo stands a big, white barn with peeling paint and crucifix windows. The hills and valleys surrounding it are plentiful with black walnut trees, fields of arugula, wildfire lettuce, retato degli ortolani melons, and the sagging branches of Matt's Wild Cherry tomato plants.

On this crisp, early fall morning, Larry Cleverley crouches to inspect frost-nipped pattypan squash. His flowing white hair shifts in the wind to reveal a bright-orange Slow Food button pinned to the breast of his faded jean jacket.

"No one knows what food is supposed to taste like," Larry says. "If they did know, they wouldn't eat the crap they eat."

He stands up to continue the casual walk from one field to the next. The sun has risen over the tree-covered hills that provide the backdrop to his farm. With each step, he gestures toward a vegetable, explaining both the value of arugula seed that's been cultivated for more than 200 years and the origins of a Mexican grape tomato.

His grandparents first purchased this land and its sandy soil, with more than 100 acres of timber, in 1928. During trying times, they would grab a cast-iron pan, a few potatoes, and some meat, and hike into the trees for their evening meal.

"It was how they got through the tough times they had," Larry explains. "They did that almost through their entire marriage. In the 1990s, when my grandmother was too old to walk, my grandfather bought a wagon for his riding lawnmower and drove her into those hills. That time together was important for both of them."

Although Larry grew up on this land, he left for a life in Chicago, and then the East Coast, where he stayed for nearly 20 years. Then, in 1996, he realized that "New York is not a town to grow old in." Upon his return to central Iowa, he took the knowledge he had gained while helping a

farmer at the 97th Street Greenmarket in Manhattan and applied it to building a reputation for growing quality food, which has made him a favorite among Iowa chefs. He favors Italian varieties because, he says, the flavors are pure and vivid, and, above all else, they taste good.

"If food doesn't taste good, what's the purpose of growing it? I'm not looking to complicate my life with customers who don't have any respect for what I do," he says, handing me a slice of ananas melon, a heartbreakingly sweet muskmelon that dates back to the 1800s. "I have total respect for [a chef's] craft and they have respect for mine."

The morning lingers on. Each slice of melon or sip of coffee is accompanied by a story of Larry's farm—a place where the fields are better kept than the house, and where this man's passion for plants is as obvious as the bright-orange button on his jacket. ∎

Rabbit Stew with Mushrooms, Kale, and Juniper Berries

SERVES 6

This comforting and spicy stew is a great way to warm up on a cool fall day. It takes four hours from start to finish, but much of that is downtime while the flavors slowly meld in the oven. Almost any type of vegetable works with this dish.

—*Jason Simon* ALBA | DES MOINES, IA

¼ cup vegetable oil

½ cup all-purpose flour

Hindquarters and forequarters of 1 rabbit

4–6 cups rabbit stock or chicken stock

12 juniper berries

12 black peppercorns

2 dried bay leaves

1 chile de arbol or ½ teaspoon ground cayenne pepper

2 yellow onions, peeled and quartered

2 carrots, peeled and cut into 2-inch pieces

2 tablespoons olive oil

12 cremini mushrooms, quartered

2 cups chopped kale

1 pint grape tomatoes, halved

Salt and freshly ground black pepper, to taste

WHERE TO FIND...

Rabbit
DeBruin Brothers
Oskaloosa, IA

Vegetables
Cleverley Farms
Mingo, IA

Preheat the oven to 275°F.

Place a large Dutch oven over medium heat and add the vegetable oil.

Place the flour onto a shallow dish. Dredge the rabbit pieces in the flour, making sure they are evenly coated.

Once the oil begins to smoke, add the rabbit and begin to brown. You may have to do this in batches. Once browned, remove the rabbit and set aside. Slowly add the stock to the Dutch oven, scraping up the brown bits.

Place the juniper berries and peppercorns into a square of cheesecloth and tie the corners together. Add the cheesecloth bundle, bay leaves, and chile de arbol to the Dutch oven. Bring to a simmer. Add the onions, carrots, and browned rabbit. Cover the Dutch oven with aluminum foil, cover the foil with the lid, and place in the oven. Cook for 3 hours.

Remove the pot from oven and let the rabbit rest in the liquid for 1 hour. After it has rested, transfer the rabbit from the liquid to a plate and set it on the countertop to finish cooling.

Remove and discard the spice bundle and bay leaves. Using an immersion blender, purée the liquid the rabbit cooked in until smooth. If you don't have an immersion blender, purée the liquid in batches in a blender, eventually returning it all to the Dutch oven. Pull the rabbit meat from the bones and add the meat to the liquid. Discard the bones.

In a medium sauté pan over medium heat, warm the olive oil. Add the mushrooms and lightly sauté until softened, but not shrunken. Add the kale and cook until it is just wilted. Add the tomatoes and sauté for 1 minute.

Transfer the vegetables to the stew. Season to taste with the salt and pepper. Reheat if necessary and serve.

Golden Potato and Cabbage Tacos with Apple–Cilantro Pico (p. 157)

Golden Potato and Cabbage Tacos with Apple–Cilantro Pico

SERVES 4 (3 TACOS PER PERSON)

Marlene's Tortilleria really makes the best corn tortillas in Nebraska. It's a real treat to eat them right out of the bag while they're still warm. If you don't get to use them right away, or are using another type of tortilla, gently warm them directly over the flame of a gas stove.

—Maggie Pleskac MAGGIE'S VEGETARIAN CAFÉ | LINCOLN, NE

TACOS

1 tablespoon cumin seeds

1 tablespoon mustard seeds

4 cups diced Yukon gold potatoes (about 6 potatoes)

6 cups sliced and crosscut green cabbage (about 1 inch thick)

3 tablespoons olive oil

2 teaspoons ground turmeric

1 teaspoon sea salt

½ teaspoon freshly ground black pepper

12 corn tortillas

APPLE-CILANTRO PICO

2 apples, finely chopped

1 cup minced fresh cilantro leaves

1 small onion, minced (about ¾ cup)

1 clove garlic, minced or pressed

Juice from ½ lime

1 teaspoon deseeded, minced jalapeño chile or ½ teaspoon red pepper flakes

½ teaspoon salt

Preheat the oven to 400°F.

In a small sauté pan over medium heat, toast the cumin and mustard seeds until they are fragrant and the mustard seeds begin to pop.

In a large bowl, combine the potatoes and cabbage. Toss with the olive oil, toasted seeds, and spices until well coated. Transfer to a baking sheet in a single layer. Roast for 20 minutes, or until evenly browned.

Meanwhile, in a large bowl, combine all the pico ingredients. Stir well.

Place some of the potato–cabbage filling into each tortilla, top with pico, and serve.

WHERE TO FIND...

Tortillas
Marlene's Tortilleria
Lincoln, NE

Yukon Gold Potatoes
Common Good Farm
Raymond, NE

Green Cabbage
Shadow Brook Farm
Lincoln, NE

Cilantro
Harvest Home
Waverly, NE

Apples
Martin's Hillside Orchard
Ceresco, NE

John Wesselius

FARMER THE CORNUCOPIA | SIOUX CENTER, IA | THECORNUCOPIACSA.COM

As a man of faith, John Wesselius believes growing food and raising animals is a spiritual endeavor. Everything is of God and for God.

John and his wife, Janna, started The Cornucopia—a 7.5-acre farm spread over three properties in Sioux County—in 2004, as both a hobby and a way to feed their own family better. At the time, Janna was a health-conscious stay-at-home mother to their four daughters, and John worked as an educational sales consultant. When his position was eliminated in 2009 due to the Great Recession, he decided it was time to fully commit to a life of selling wholesome food and sharing agricultural philosophy.

"I really believe we are stewards of the creation. We are all responsible for taking care of it. Sometimes it means making choices about certain farming practices. Sometimes it means speaking out; sometimes it means biting your tongue. It's all part of the physiological and spiritual rhythms that have been set in place before this," John says. He walks toward the barn, past the rows of rhubarb announcing their seasonal sacrifice with sturdy stalks of ivory flowers going to seed; he continues past the sheets printed with conversation hearts dangling on the clothesline.

Like any man of faith, he feels he has been tested. It would've been easier to take a job in town than to work the soil. There would be no need to worry about the weather or if a windstorm will destroy the infrastructure used to extend the growing season.

An office job might give him Saturdays off, but it wouldn't feed his soul or his sense of purpose.

"Food, unfortunately, has become a commodity," John explains. "When food appears so plentiful, yet even in small wealthy towns children are food-insecure, or are consuming calories but not nutrients, we should ask why. What if we considered eating food a sacrament? What if we treasured food?"

Despite feeling at times like the path toward success is longer than anticipated, he finds comfort in his faith, the strength of his family, his farm, and the community he serves with his produce.

"I have come to believe that despite sometimes going two steps forward and one step backward, despite the difficulties, that this is a calling," John continues in his honest and frank communication style. "It's a matter of confidence. It's a matter of knowing that God is always in control. It doesn't matter what happens; ultimately, we are taken care of. We are provided for." ▪

Braised Bison Short Ribs

SERVES 6

Braising is a simple and relatively hands-off way to make a delicious meal. Bison goes especially well with mashed or roasted potatoes and good fall vegetables like parsnips, turnips, brussels sprouts, squash, and sweet potatoes. Start this dish about four hours before you want to serve it, so you have time to reduce the braising liquid.

—*Michael Haskett* M.B. HASKETT DELICATESSEN | SIOUX FALLS, SD

4 slices bacon, cut into short strips

3 pounds bison short ribs

Salt and freshly ground black pepper, to taste

1 bulb garlic (skin on)

1 large onion, roughly chopped

2 carrots, roughly chopped

3 ribs celery, roughly chopped

2 tablespoons tomato paste

¼ cup all-purpose flour

2 cups red wine

6 cups beef or bison stock

3 sprigs fresh thyme

1 sprig fresh rosemary

2 fresh bay leaves

3 tablespoons butter, chilled

WHERE TO FIND...

Bison
Wild Idea Buffalo Co.
Rapid City, SD

Carrots, Onion, Herbs
Linda's Gardens
Chester, SD

Garlic
Prairie Coteau Farm
Astoria, SD

Preheat the oven to 325°F.

In a large sauté pan over medium heat, cook the bacon.

Meanwhile, pat the short ribs dry with a paper towel and season lightly with the salt and pepper. Break the garlic bulb into cloves, leaving the skin on.

When the bacon is crisp, remove it from the pan with a slotted spoon and let drain on a paper towel. Leave the rendered fat in the pan and save the bacon for another day. (You need only the fat for this recipe.) Add the ribs to the pan and sear on all sides until nicely browned. (You may need to do this in batches.) Transfer the ribs to a Dutch oven or large, heavy braising dish that can go from the stovetop to the oven.

Drain off any excess fat from the pan, leaving just enough to cook the vegetables. Add the vegetables and garlic cloves to the hot pan, stirring occasionally to scrape up the good meat drippings from the bottom of the pan. When the vegetables are nicely browned, stir in the tomato paste and cook long enough to get rid of the raw tomato flavor, about 2 minutes. Sprinkle the flour over the vegetables and stir. Cook for about 1 more minute. Add the red wine and stir, scraping up any remaining flavor bits stuck to the bottom of the pan. When the wine has simmered for about 5 minutes, add the stock. Once the stock is warm, carefully pour the entire pan, vegetables and all, over the ribs in the Dutch oven. Add the thyme, rosemary, and bay leaves, and a small sprinkle of the salt and pepper. Cover with aluminum foil and a lid to keep the liquid from escaping. Place in the oven and cook for 3 hours.

Wash the sauté pan you browned the bison in and return it to the stove. You will use it to reduce the braising liquid later.

After 3 hours, check the meat. A fork should be able to slide into the meat, and the meat should shred when the fork is twisted. Have a little taste. If the meat is still chewy, give the ribs another 30 to 45 minutes. If the meat falls off the bone when you remove a rib from the pan, it is done.

Remove the ribs from the braising liquid and set aside. Pour the liquid through a strainer and into the washed sauté pan. Discard the solids. Bring the braising liquid to a simmer over medium heat. Use a ladle to remove any grease and impurities that rise to the top. This will take about 30 minutes.

Shred the meat. When the sauce is reduced to a gravy-like consistency, turn off the heat and whisk in the cold butter. Season to taste with the salt and pepper. Stir the shredded meat into the sauce. Serve.

Butternut Squash Pie with Cinnamon Whole-Grain Crust

SERVES 8

This recipe came about when I realized I was out of pumpkin but I still needed to make pie. I used butternut squash in place of pumpkin in my pie recipe, and it actually worked out better.

The crust is more substantial than your typical piecrust, and is prone to cracking, so take care when rolling it out.

—*Kristine Moberg* QUEEN CITY BAKERY | SIOUX FALLS, SD

CRUST

¾ cup rolled oats

⅓ cup all-purpose flour, plus more for rolling

¼ cup whole-wheat flour

3 tablespoons packed brown sugar

¾ teaspoon ground cinnamon

¼ teaspoon kosher salt

6½ tablespoons butter, chilled and cubed

2–3 tablespoons whole milk, cold

FILLING

1 3-pound butternut squash

Oil, for roasting the squash

½ cup plus 1 tablespoon heavy cream

2 tablespoons maple syrup

⅓ cup packed brown sugar

¾ teaspoon ground cinnamon

¾ teaspoon ground ginger

¾ teaspoon kosher salt

⅛ teaspoon ground cloves

⅛ teaspoon ground nutmeg

⅛ teaspoon freshly ground black pepper

2 eggs

1 egg yolk

Whipped cream, for serving

TO MAKE THE CRUST

Place the rolled oats in a food processor and process for 30 to 45 seconds. Add the flours, sugar, cinnamon, and salt and pulse until combined.

Add the butter cubes and pulse until they are in pea-sized pieces and the dough looks crumbly, like coarse sand. Gradually add the milk and pulse until combined. The dough will be loose. Turn the dough out onto a sheet of plastic wrap. Form a ball with the dough, wrap it in the plastic wrap, and press it into a fat disk. Chill in the refrigerator for at least 3 hours.

Preheat the oven to 375°F.

Lightly flour your countertop and roll out the dough, dusting as needed so it doesn't stick. (If it's too difficult to roll out, let it sit at room temperature for 10 minutes or so.) This dough is a bit temperamental and can split, so be patient. Gently fold the dough over your rolling pin, pick it up, and place it into a 9-inch pie pan. Form it to the pan. Prick the bottom of the crust with a fork a few times. Place parchment paper on top of the crust and fill it with pie weights. If you don't have weights, just pour some dried beans onto the parchment. Bake the weighted crust for 20 minutes. Remove the crust from the oven, remove the weights and parchment, and bake the crust for 5 more minutes. Remove it from the oven and make your filling while it cools. Keep the oven on and at 375°F for roasting the squash.

TO MAKE THE FILLING AND BAKE THE PIE

Split the squash down the middle. Scoop out the seeds and lightly oil the flesh. Place the cut sides down on a baking sheet and roast until tender, about 45 minutes to 1 hour, depending on the size. Once roasted and cool to the touch, scoop the flesh into your food processor or blender and purée. You need only 1¼ cups of roasted squash for this recipe, but the remainder freezes well and can be used to make pie the next time you have a craving.

In a large bowl, whisk together the squash purée, cream, and maple syrup.

WHERE TO FIND...

Squash
The Cornucopia
Sioux Center, IA

Dairy
Burbach's Countryside Dairy
Hartington, NE

In a small bowl, mix together the brown sugar and spices, then whisk the spice mixture into the squash mixture. Whisk in the eggs and yolk. Pour the mixture into the prepared pie crust. Make an aluminum foil ring to cover the edge of the crust. Bake for 35 to 40 minutes, until the center has just a slight jiggle. Cool to room temperature. Serve with the whipped cream.

Winter

Dried Fruit and Pumpkin Seed Granola

MAKES ABOUT 3½ POUNDS

This easy-to-make granola will fill your kitchen with the sweet, comforting scents of cinnamon and honey. Total baking time is 35 to 40 minutes, so stay close and stir every 10 minutes. Enjoy on its own, with milk, or sprinkled on yogurt.

—*Kristine Moberg* QUEEN CITY BAKERY | SIOUX FALLS, SD

7 cups rolled oats

¾ cup packed brown sugar

½ cup honey

⅓ cup safflower oil, plus more to oil your hands

¼ cup maple syrup

1½ teaspoons ground cinnamon

1½ teaspoons vanilla extract

¾ teaspoon kosher salt

1 cup chopped pecans

¾ cup shelled pumpkin seeds (pepitas)

1 cup golden raisins

1 cup dried cranberries

WHERE TO FIND...

Honey
Deep Creek Honey
Hartford, SD

Preheat the oven to 325°F. Line a large baking sheet with parchment paper.

Place the oats in a large bowl. Set aside.

In a medium bowl, whisk together the sugar, honey, oil, maple syrup, cinnamon, vanilla extract, and salt. Pour this mixture over the oats. Oil your hands and start mixing everything together. Make sure all the oats are coated.

Spread the mixture onto the prepared baking sheet and bake for 10 minutes. Stir the granola and bake for another 10 minutes. Stir in the pecans and pumpkin seeds and bake for another 10 minutes. Stir the granola and bake for 5 to 10 more minutes. The color should be golden. If it's not, stir and continue to bake, 10 minutes at a time, until it is.

Remove the granola from the oven. Let cool completely before mixing and adding in the raisins and cranberries. This simple snack will store well in an airtight container for up to 2 weeks.

Note: If your baking sheet isn't large enough, split the batch between 2 sheets and rotate them top to bottom in the oven every time you stir the granola. You want the granola to be dry and crunchy once it cools, not chewy.

Kristine Moberg and Mitch Jackson

BAKERS QUEEN CITY BAKERY | 324 E. 8TH ST. | SIOUX FALLS, SD |
605.274.6060 | WWW.QUEENCITYBAKERY.COM

Kristine Moberg and Mitch Jackson left New York City as a fading image in the rearview mirror of their rented moving truck. With little more than a name and a rough sketch of a logo, their plan was to open a from-scratch bakery featuring classic American desserts and breakfast items in their home state of South Dakota.

They arrived in Sioux Falls and moved in with Mitch's parents while they saved money, wrote a business plan, scouted for locations, and developed recipes. Within seven months of their return, Queen City Bakery opened its doors and started serving luscious, moist layer cakes; brioche; and granola to all who entered.

"When we decided to open the bakery, we were all business from the very beginning," said Mitch, who spoke from his home while their son, Luca, played in the background. "My wife is very schedule oriented. We had a meeting every day at eight a.m. at the kitchen table. It wasn't a 'come in your pajamas and sip coffee' meeting—it was a 'get dressed, we are going to work' meeting. We knew we didn't want to move back to South Dakota to work for someone else."

Kristine didn't intend to become a baker. When she lived in France, where she met Mitch, she was teaching English, not practicing the art of a perfectly layered dacquoise. Later, when they moved to New York City, she simply wanted a job and thought the Polka Dot Cake Studio looked like a nice place to work. She started by making lattes and helping customers in the front of the house; by the time she left, she was in the kitchen full time, and, most importantly, she was baking.

Her next stop, the final one before she and Mitch opened their own place, was Baked, the famed Brooklyn pastry shop where she honed her skills and made multiple appearances on the *Martha Stewart Show*.

"Up until my time at Polka Dot, I was switching ideas on what I wanted to do with my life," says Kristine, who has a bachelor's degree in kinesiology, the study of human movement. "The bakery work connected with me. It was just a good fit for my personality. I'm very meticulous, organized, and detail oriented. I picked it up quickly and was good at it."

RECIPES FROM KRISTINE:

› Roasted Asparagus Quiche (p. 14)

› 24K Carrot Cake with Cream Cheese Frosting (p. 100)

› Butternut Squash Pie with Cinnamon Whole-Grain Crust (p. 162)

› Dried Fruit and Pumpkin Seed Granola (p. 167)

Since opening Queen City Bakery in 2008, they have moved to a larger location, two blocks west of the original spot, in the East Bank district of downtown Sioux Falls. Kristine says they don't have plans to further expand the bakery, though people often encourage them to offer lunch items. If anything, she says, they will continue to improve upon their current offerings.

"Maybe it's just accomplishment enough to have a family and keep the business consistent. It's something I'm always concerned about," she says. "I want the person who visits us once a month to enjoy the same quality oatmeal, fruit, and nut cookie each time they come in our door." ■

Ham, Chile, and Cheddar Egg Strata

SERVES 12

Our daughter, Ellen, makes strata at least twice a week at the bakery. It is a great way to use leftover bread. You can assemble this the night before, put it in the refrigerator, and bake it the next morning, but we just pop it right in the oven the same day.

—*Charlotte and John Hamburger* BACK ALLEY BAKERY | HASTINGS, NE

1 pound sourdough bread, cubed, divided (about 6 cups)

2 cups shredded cheddar cheese, divided

1 cup cubed ham (½-inch cubes), divided

2 4-ounce cans diced mild green chilies (undrained), divided

8 eggs

4 cups whole milk

1½ teaspoons salt

½ teaspoon freshly ground black pepper

WHERE TO FIND...

Eggs
Donna Faimon
Lawrence, NE

Cheese
Clear Creek Organic Farms
Spalding, NE

Preheat the oven to 350°F.

Butter a 9 × 13-inch baking pan. In layers, add ½ pound of the bread, 1 cup of the cheese, ½ cup of the ham, and 1 can of the chilies to the pan. Repeat with the remaining bread, cheese, ham, and chilies.

In a large bowl, whisk together the eggs, milk, salt, and pepper. Pour over the bread mixture in the baking pan. Bake for 60 to 70 minutes, until a knife comes out clean. Put the pan under the broiler for about 1 to 2 minutes to crisp the top. Serve and enjoy.

Roasted Heirloom Beet Terrine

SERVES 8

Come winter, root vegetables are scary good. The frost and cool soil help consolidate sugar in the roots as the green vegetation dies back. In Nebraska, where frosts typically arrive in October, but the days can stay sunny, root vegetables take on a marvelous dimension that can continue into the winter months, depending upon the year. Here, beets are featured, but they can easily be replaced with turnips, carrots, parsnips, or rutabagas.

—Paul Kulik THE BOILER ROOM | OMAHA, NE

1 pound red beets

1 pound chioggia beets

1 pound yellow beets

3 tablespoons olive oil, plus more for brushing

4 cloves garlic, minced

¼ teaspoon ground cayenne pepper, plus more for garnish

Salt, to taste

2 cups chicken stock

3 large leeks (whites only), washed and sliced

Pumpkin seed oil, for garnish

Fresh, tender, leafy herbs (such as tarragon or chervil), for garnish

8 slices prosciutto

WHERE TO FIND...

Beets
Shadow Brook Farm
Lincoln, NE

Prosciutto
La Quercia
Norwalk, IA

Preheat the oven to 325°F.

Trim the beet tops and ends, but leave the skin on. Tear enough pieces of aluminum foil to wrap each beet individually, and set the beets in the center of each piece of foil. Coat the beets with the olive oil and season with the garlic, cayenne pepper, and salt to taste. Wrap the beets up and bake until tender, about 45 minutes to 1 hour.

In a large pot, bring the chicken stock to a boil. Add the leek whites and poach until tender. Remove from the heat and set aside to cool.

If you have a heavy terrine mold, use it; if not, 2 loaf pans (8 inch or otherwise) and 5 15-ounce cans (unopened) will work. You just need something to help compress the beets. Line the mold with plastic wrap, leaving some of the plastic hanging over the edge on all sides.

Remove the beets from the oven. Cool a bit, then unwrap and peel them by rubbing the skin off with a towel. Evenly and thinly slice the beets and then layer in the mold. Gently brush each layer with some of the olive oil and lightly season with the salt. Take care to group the beets together by color, because the colors will bleed.

When halfway up the mold, place a layer of leeks from end to end, then continue adding layers of the beets. When full, pull the plastic wrap tightly over the top and side of the beets. Top with a 5-pound weight to press it together, or set a second loaf pan on top of the beets and fill it with the cans. Chill in the refrigerator for a minimum of 24 hours.

To serve, open the plastic wrap and invert the beets onto a plate. Remove the plastic wrap. Using a sharp knife, slice at the desired width. Put each slice on a plate and drizzle with the pumpkin seed oil. Add a slight sprinkle of cayenne pepper around the plate. Top with a small amount of tender herbs. Add a rosette of prosciutto to the side of the beets and serve.

Note: If you want to use parsnips instead of beets, slice them lengthwise to ¼ inch thick. Boil the slices until tender in salted water, rather than roasting them, to keep the white color. Alternate with carrot slices, cooked the same way. Trim the tips so they fit the width of the pan, placing the wide end of one parsnip next to the narrow end of another so they are snug. Brush each layer with the oil and season with the salt and pepper.

Benjamin Smart

CHEF BIG GROVE BREWERY | 101 W. MAIN ST. | SOLON, IA | 319.624.2337 |
WWW.BIGGROVEBREWERY.COM

RECIPES FROM BENJAMIN:

> Lavender-Crusted Rack of Lamb
  with Asparagus, Morel Ragù, and
  Potato Purée (p. 39)

> Open-Faced Caponata and Heirloom
  Tomato Sandwich (p. 77)

> Mushroom Focaccia with Shallots,
  Savory, and Olive Oil (p. 112)

> Crispy Fingerling Potato Salad with
  Stone-Ground Mustard Vinaigrette
  (p.174)

In the life of every craftsman, there is a moment when he plunges into the depths of his trade, when style collides with substance and embraces mission and meaning. For Benjamin Smart, executive chef at Big Grove Brewery in Solon, that moment came when a chance encounter at a Kansas City, Missouri, restaurant taught him that creating delicious food wasn't enough; it had to be meaningful.

In 2008, Benjamin was a line cook at the American when Keith Luce visited as guest chef for an event to support Share Our Strength, a nonprofit organization dedicated to ending childhood hunger. At the time, Luce was the chef at the famed Herbfarm, a pioneering farm-to-table restaurant in Woodinville, Washington.

"He was amazing," says Benjamin. "Not only because of the level and beauty of the food, but because he knew when the radish was at its best because it still had its sugars and hadn't been fully converted to starch yet."

Within eight weeks, Benjamin was on staff at the Herbfarm, which is located on a five-and-a-half-acre working farm where they raise pigs, fowl, and produce, while immersing promising chefs in local food culture and philosophy.

"We dried the field corn, ground it, and made it into polenta. When you do that, take something from beginning to end, you look at food differently and you cook it differently," Benjamin says. He stands poised and upright. His long fingers are wrapped loosely around the neck strap of his blue-and-white denim Hedley & Bennett apron. "That is where my food philosophy started taking hold; it's where I evolved from focusing solely on technique."

After spending five years at the Herbfarm, Benjamin and his wife decided it was time to move back to his home state of Iowa. The perfect opportunity came when Doug Goettsch, a family friend, contacted Benjamin and explained the concept for a new craft brewery and restaurant in Solon. Doug and his business partner, Matt Swift, needed a chef who could highlight the great produce of the region and elevate the food. He hoped Benjamin might have a recommendation or two. Benjamin recommended himself, and five months later he left the West Coast for Iowa with his pregnant wife and young daughter. A few months after that, Big Grove Brewery opened with Benjamin's innovative approach to modern American Midwest comfort food.

"A lot of people think we are meat-and-potatoes people and we don't know how to cook or appreciate anything else. I have the room here to flex a little bit of muscle. I'm not making fine-dining food. There aren't any flower garnishes, but good food is good food. If you offer that quality to people and present it to them in a way they will accept, they will flip for it. So far, it's proven to be true," says Benjamin. ∎

"When you do that, take something from beginning to end, you look at food differently and you cook it differently."

Crispy Fingerling Potato Salad with Stone-Ground Mustard Vinaigrette

SERVES 4

Much of this hearty salad can be made a day or two in advance and treated as an entrée. It's best to pickle the onion a day before you want to eat the salad, but if you forget, it will still taste great. The pickled onion will keep for up to two weeks. The dressing uses raw egg yolk and will be good for up to three days. Grapeseed oil provides a unique, nutty flavor to the potatoes, but whatever you have on hand will also work.

—Benjamin Smart BIG GROVE BREWERY | SOLON, IA

PICKLED RED ONION

1 cup red wine vinegar

1 cup water

¼ cup granulated sugar

2 tablespoons salt

1 red onion (core removed), julienned

STONE-GROUND MUSTARD VINAIGRETTE

¼ cup fresh lemon juice

2 egg yolks

1 tablespoon stone-ground mustard

1 teaspoon honey

1 teaspoon minced shallots

¾ cup extra virgin olive oil

Salt, to taste

TO MAKE THE PICKLED ONION

In a medium saucepan, bring the vinegar, water, sugar, and salt to a rolling boil. Add the onion, reduce the heat to a gentle simmer, and then remove the saucepan from the heat. Let the onion cool to room temperature in the pickling liquid. You can store the pickled onion (in its liquid) in the refrigerator for up to 2 weeks.

TO MAKE THE VINAIGRETTE

In a small bowl, combine the lemon juice, egg yolks, mustard, honey, and shallots. While whisking constantly, slowly add the olive oil in a steady stream to form an emulsified vinaigrette. Season to taste with the salt. Set aside.

TO MAKE THE POTATOES AND ASSEMBLE THE SALAD

Bring a large pot of water to a rolling boil. Set a bowl of ice water nearby. Add the eggs to the boiling water and cook for 8 to 9 minutes. Transfer the eggs to the bowl of ice water to stop the cooking process. Once cool, peel the eggs and quarter them lengthwise. The egg white should be hard-cooked, and the yolk should be firm, but still a bit jammy. Season to taste with the sea salt.

Rinse out the pot in which you boiled the eggs, then place the potatoes, garlic, bay leaves, and thyme sprigs in it. Cover with water and season aggressively with the table salt—it should almost taste like the ocean. Bring to a simmer and cook (never letting the water boil) for 20 minutes, or until the potatoes are fork-tender. Drain the water and let the potatoes cool to room temperature. Once cool, gently press on each potato with the palm of your hand, flattening it but allowing the skin of the potato to hold it together in 1 piece.

POTATO SALAD

4 eggs

Sea salt, to taste

2 pounds fingerling potatoes

4 cloves garlic

2 bay leaves, preferably fresh

2 sprigs fresh thyme

Table salt, for cooking the
potatoes

½ cup grapeseed oil

8 white anchovy fillets, cured in
olive oil (optional)

12 paper-thin slices prosciutto,
for garnish

Chopped fresh tarragon, chives,
and dill, for garnish

WHERE TO FIND...

Eggs
Kroul Farms
Mount Vernon, IA

Prosciutto
La Quercia
Norwalk, IA

Vegetables
Wild Woods Farm
Solon, IA

In a large sauté pan, heat the grapeseed oil over medium–high heat until it is just beginning to smoke. Cook the smashed potatoes in a single layer until golden brown on both sides; they should be quite crispy. You may have to do this in batches. Drain on a plate lined with paper towels and season to taste with the sea salt.

If using the anchovies, warm a grill pan over medium–high heat. Grill the anchovies gently on one side, just allowing the skin to attain a grill mark, but not so much that the fish sticks or falls apart, about 1 minute. Remove from the heat and set aside.

In a large bowl, place the potatoes and lightly dress with about 2 tablespoons of the vinaigrette. (You will have extra vinaigrette; it will keep in the refrigerator for up to 3 days.) Divide evenly among 4 plates. Garnish with the thinly shaved prosciutto, 2 grilled anchovies, the cooked egg, the pickled onion, and lots of fresh herbs.

Kate Edwards

FARMER WILD WOODS FARM | SOLON, IA | WWW.WILDWOODSCSA.COM

Kate Edwards walks with her hands tucked into the front pockets of her jeans. The tails of her blue-and-ivory western-wear shirt with pearl-snap buttons billow in the wet air. She opens the door to the germination house located on ZJ Farm, owned by her friend and mentor, Susan Jutz. Inside the semicircular structure made of plastic and concrete, wood trays of eggplant, mustard greens, and bok choy await their summer home at Kate's Wild Woods Farm, 10 miles due south.

While childhood experiences on her grandparents' farm inspired Kate's life in agriculture, it was Susan who provided the encouragement, resources, and practical training necessary to live successfully off the land. Susan and Kate are in the bedroom community of Solon, only a 20-minute drive to the metropolitan areas of Iowa City and Cedar Rapids—a nearly perfect geographic placement for a local food supplier.

"I consider it an incredible privilege to call myself a farmer."

In 2008, Kate earned her master's degree in agricultural engineering and began her career as a farmer two years later. She supplies produce to a handful of restaurants and feeds more than 150 families through her CSA program. In less than three years, her operation was self-funded. Although she leases her land presently, she hopes to purchase farm ground when the perfect place is available at the right price. She equates her success to personal drive as well as good mentors who are willing to share generational knowledge.

Kate and Susan met briefly years ago, but their friendship didn't begin until they connected in 2011 at a farm tour hosted by Susan and Practical Farmers of Iowa, a farmer-led nonprofit organization dedicated to advancing profitable, ecologically sound, and community-enhancing approaches to agriculture.

"She came up to me and said, 'We need more people like you in this business. We need more women and we need more young farmers,'" Kate explains as she meanders down the rows of the germination house, a space she shares with three other female farmers. She points to the

trays, each bold with texture and color—the purple edges of a weeks-old red mustard plant, and the frail, blade-like appearance of a new eggplant seedling. She brushes the palm of her hand across the tops of these plants as she describes them in their various stages of development.

"Sometimes we joke because I'm stubborn, but it's nice to have someone who has gone before you to show you the steps," Kate says just before plucking the leaf of a baby lettuce to sample. A gentle smile spreads across her face and she pauses for a second. "I never thought I would be smart enough or have the opportunity to do this," she continues. "I consider it an incredible privilege to call myself a farmer." ■

Creamy Potato Soup with Braised Oxtail and Citrus

SERVES 8 (1 CUP PER PERSON) OR 4 (2 CUPS PER PERSON)

When I was growing up in this wonderful state of Nebraska, my mother made potato soup every winter. The soup usually consisted of a beef broth made with the roast beef from the night before, trimmings from the same roast beef, and a ton of potatoes, carrots, onions, and anything else that was in the fridge. This recipe pays homage to that soup, but with a slight variation. Instead of using a broth base, the soup is buttermilk and potato based. The blood orange adds brightness to the hearty soup, and the oxtail is a nice variation of the roast beef I remember eating as a child.

This soup has multiple components and should be started 24 to 48 hours ahead of time. Prior to cooking each component, prep everything you need, as it comes together quickly. If you cannot find cipollini onions, pearl onions also work in this dish. If using pearl onions, serve four per bowl.

—*Clayton Chapman* THE GREY PLUME | OMAHA, NE

BRAISED OXTAIL

1 oxtail

2 cups red wine

Kosher salt and freshly ground black pepper, to taste

¼ cup vegetable oil

2 cups diced onion (½-inch dice)

1 cup peeled and diced carrot (½-inch dice)

1 cup diced celery (½-inch dice)

3 cups beef broth

3 sprigs fresh thyme

1 fresh bay leaf

2 blood oranges

TO MAKE THE OXTAIL

In a deep, nonreactive dish, place the oxtail and cover it with the wine. The oxtail should be completely submerged. Transfer the dish to the refrigerator and let the oxtail marinate for 8 to 12 hours. Once marinated, remove the oxtail and reserve the liquid. Pat the oxtail dry with paper towels and season with the salt and pepper.

Preheat the oven to 250°F.

Set a large Dutch oven over medium heat and add the vegetable oil. Sear the oxtail on all sides. Transfer the oxtail from the Dutch oven to a plate and set nearby. Add the diced onion, carrot, and celery to the Dutch oven and sauté until you develop a nice dark color on the exterior of the vegetables. This could take close to 25 minutes. Once the vegetables are done, add the reserved red wine, beef broth, thyme sprigs, and bay leaf and bring to a boil. Add the oxtail. Remove from the heat, cover with a lid, and braise in the oven for 12 hours, or until the oxtail comes off the bone easily. It's critical that the lid fit the pot securely so that very little moisture is released. You may need to cover your pot with aluminum foil before placing on the lid to ensure a tight fit.

Meanwhile, zest the oranges and set the zest aside. Segment each orange by cutting a little off the top and the bottom (so it stands on end without rolling). The goal is to remove the skin and the pith, while leaving most of the flesh intact. After the top and bottom are removed and the color of the orange is exposed, start cutting down the sides, following the curve of the fruit. You should see the reddish-orange flesh. Remove and discard the pith and skin. Using a paring knife, cut the individual segments of fruit from the membrane. After segmenting all the fruit, set the segments aside.

POTATO SOUP

2 pounds Yukon gold potatoes, peeled and cut into 1-inch pieces

3 cups whole milk

1 yellow onion, julienned

3 sprigs fresh thyme

1–1½ cups buttermilk

½ cup chopped spinach (stems removed)

⅓ cup plus 1 tablespoon George Paul red wine vinegar

Kosher salt and freshly ground black pepper, to taste

CIPOLLINI ONIONS

2 tablespoons vegetable oil

8 cipollini onions, peeled and halved (root end still intact)

2 tablespoons unsalted butter

1 sprig fresh thyme

Kosher salt and freshly ground black pepper, to taste

2 tablespoons cold water

1 tablespoon George Paul red wine vinegar

Chopped fresh chives or parsley, to taste

WHERE TO FIND...

Potatoes
Honey Creek Farms
Oakland, IA

Cipollini Onions
Rhizosphere Farm
Missouri Valley, IA

Oxtail
Majinola Meats
Panama, IA

Dairy
Burbach's Countryside Dairy
Hartington, NE

Vinegar
George Paul Vinegar
Cody, NE

When the oxtail has finished braising, remove it from the oven. Take care when removing the lid and/or foil from the Dutch oven; it will release hot steam. Remove the oxtail from the braising liquid and set aside in a bowl.

Set a strainer over a saucepan and pour the liquid from the Dutch oven through it. Discard the solids caught in strainer. If you feel the liquid in the saucepan is too oily, skim off some of the oil with a spoon. Over medium heat, reduce the braising liquid by ¾.

While the meat is still warm, use your fingers to separate the meat from the fat and bone. Once the liquid is reduced, pour as much of the braising liquid as needed over the meat to moisten it without making it soupy. Fold in the orange zest. If you have extra braising liquid, pour it into ice cube trays and freeze it to use as a beef stock base another day.

TO MAKE THE POTATO SOUP

In a large pot, place the potatoes, whole milk, onion, and thyme sprigs. Make sure the potatoes are completely submerged. Cook over medium heat until the potatoes are fork-tender, about 20 minutes. Add the buttermilk. Continue to cook until the potatoes are soft enough to blend, about 15 minutes more. Remove from the heat, then remove and discard the thyme sprigs. Using a blender or an immersion blender, blend the mixture until smooth. If you would like the soup thinner, add more buttermilk. Stir in the spinach and vinegar. Season to taste with the salt and pepper. Set aside.

TO MAKE THE ONIONS AND ASSEMBLE THE DISH

In a medium sauté pan, heat the oil over medium heat and add the cipollini onions. Sear until they get a nice crust on one side. Strain the oil out of the pan. Add the butter and thyme sprig and season to taste with the salt and pepper. Continue to sauté the onions until the butter foams, then add the cold water. Reduce until the water evaporates. Add the red wine vinegar. Season to taste again with the salt and pepper. Add the fresh chives or parsley. Set aside.

To serve, place a small amount of braised oxtail in the bottom of each bowl. Add 4 onion halves and 3 blood orange segments. When ready to serve, pour the hot potato soup over the top.

Rice- and Kale-Stuffed Squash with Pecan Gomashio

SERVES 4 (OR 8 IF QUARTERED)

Stuffing just makes sense in the winter. Even the term itself sounds warm and cozy.

Gomashio is an Asian condiment typically used as a topping and made of toasted sesame seeds and salt. Pecans add a touch of winter to this gomashio.

This recipe is gluten free, soy free, dairy free, and egg free. You can substitute other grains for the rice, such as quinoa. This dish makes for an easy and healthy weeknight meal.

—*Maggie Pleskac* MAGGIE'S VEGETARIAN CAFÉ | LINCOLN, NE

SQUASH

2 acorn squash

1 tablespoon olive oil, plus more for baking

1 teaspoon sea salt, plus more for sprinkling

Freshly ground black pepper

2 tablespoons minced onion

½ tablespoon minced garlic (about 2 cloves)

1 cup basmati rice

1 tablespoon nutritional yeast powder or flakes (optional)

2 cups water

2 cups chopped and packed kale

Chopped fresh parsley, for garnish

GOMASHIO

¼ cup pecans

¼ cup sesame seeds

½ teaspoon sea salt

WHERE TO FIND...

Acorn Squash
Common Good Farm
Raymond, NE

Kale
Robinette Farms
Martell, NE

Pecans
Heartland Nuts 'N More
Valparaiso, NE

TO MAKE THE SQUASH

Preheat the oven to 400°F.

Halve the squash and remove the seeds. Rub a little oil on the flesh of each squash half; sprinkle with the salt and pepper. Place the squash cut side down on a baking sheet and bake for 40 minutes, or until you can easily pierce the flesh with a fork.

Meanwhile, prepare the rice. In a large saucepan, warm the olive oil over medium heat. Add the onion and garlic and sauté for 3 minutes, or until softened. Add the rice, nutritional yeast (if using), and salt. Stir well to coat the rice. Add the water. Cover the pan and bring to a boil, then reduce to a simmer and cook for 20 minutes, or until the water is absorbed and the rice is soft. When the rice has about 10 minutes left to cook, put the chopped kale on top of the rice and cover. When the rice is finished cooking, stir to combine it with the kale.

TO MAKE THE GOMASHIO AND ASSEMBLE THE DISH

While the rice and squash cook, prepare the gomashio. Toast the pecans and sesame seeds in a dry sauté pan until just fragrant and beginning to brown. Remove from the heat and transfer to a food processor. Add the salt and pulse for about 30 seconds, until the mixture is a coarse meal.

When the squash halves are warm enough to handle, fill each half with the rice mixture and sprinkle with the gomashio. Garnish with the fresh parsley. Serve.

Jason Simon

CHEF ALBA | 524 E. 6TH ST. | DES MOINES, IA | 515.244.0261 | WWW.ALBADSM.COM

RECIPES FROM JASON:

› Spring Garlic Soup (p. 27)

› Caramelized Pattypan Squash Salad with Summer Peaches (p. 66)

› Rabbit Stew with Mushrooms, Kale, and Juniper Berries (p. 152)

› Potato and Squash Gratin (p. 186)

Upon entering Alba, a James Beard Award–nominated contemporary American restaurant in the East Village area of Des Moines, you are likely to notice three things: curved walls, old doors hanging from the ceiling, and, depending upon the night, a small roving action figure.

Chef and owner Jason Simon, world traveler and native of Parkersburg, returned to his home state to open Alba in 2008. Putting his heart into the restaurant translates into taking nothing for granted. He values a good cup of coffee, a good day, and, perhaps most of all, a good meal shared with those he holds dear.

"When you see the world, you realize what is important to you," says Jason, casually touching the red braided bracelet on his wrist, a treasure from a trip to South America. "I have a strong relationship with my parents and my family. The experiences away were great, but it was time to come home."

You don't have to visit with Jason for long to realize that he is a methodical man. He will straighten tables, brush crumbs, and place elements on a plate with exacting detail. He expects the same care and consideration from the farmers whose products he uses to build Alba's menu.

"I think what local producers do is an amazing art," Jason says, sipping water from a red Nalgene bottle. "They have to know their own cycles to be a successful farmer. It's a tough business. They can't control what happens in the outside world. I guess you could say there is a nurturing spirit to it. You can tell the difference between someone who puts a lot of love into their work and someone who puts nothing into it. It's obvious."

Each component of the restaurant represents a piece of Jason. The curved walls pull energy through the space, mimicking the rounded corners of the building's original 1950s facade. The connection of the outside structure to the inside speaks to his eye for detail. His resourcefulness is apparent in the old doors suspended from the ceiling, as they help improve acoustics. And the roaming superhero action figure—well, that's simply about having a good time. ∎

Potato and Squash Gratin

SERVES 8

This dish uses just about every part of the squash, including the peels. While this version is served family style in a large dish, the presentation can be dressed up a bit by preparing it in individual ramekins.

—*Jason Simon* ALBA | DES MOINES, IA

2 tablespoons butter, plus more
for greasing

3 Yukon gold potatoes

½ butternut squash

1½ cups heavy cream

3 tablespoons honey

3 tablespoons soy sauce

3 egg yolks

½ cup grated parmesan cheese

WHERE TO FIND...

Potatoes
Maxwell Farms
State Center, IA

Preheat the oven to 350°F. Grease the inside of an 8 × 8-inch baking dish with butter.

Wash and peel the potatoes, reserving the peels. Set aside.

Wash the squash. Remove and discard 1 inch off the top and the bottom. Using a vegetable peeler, and working away from yourself, peel the squash until you reach the deep-orange flesh. Remove and discard the seeds, but reserve the peels. Set aside.

Fill a large bowl with cold water and set nearby. Using a mandoline slicer, slice the potatoes and squash paper thin, then transfer the slices to the bowl of water.

In a large pot, heat the cream, honey, soy sauce, and reserved squash and potato peels over medium heat and cook until the liquid has reduced by ⅓, about 30 minutes. Add the butter. Pour the mixture into a blender and blend until smooth.

In a bowl large enough to hold the cream mixture, place the egg yolks. Whisk the yolks continuously while slowly pouring the warm liquid into the bowl. The goal is to temper, not cook, the eggs.

In the prepared baking dish, place the potatoes and squash in alternating layers (potato, then squash, then potato, and so on), slightly overlapping each layer. Once a layer is finished, add just enough of the cream mixture to cover the vegetables. Repeat this process until all of the vegetables are used. Place the baking dish on top of a baking sheet to catch drips. Cover the baking dish with aluminum foil and bake for about 45 minutes to 1 hour. Remove from the oven, remove the foil, and top with the parmesan cheese. Change the oven setting to broil. Cook under the broiler for another 5 to 7 minutes, until the cheese is browned on top.

Remove from the oven. Let the gratin rest for about 15 minutes before serving.

Braised Rabbit with Cipollini Onions and Creamy White Polenta

SERVES 4

This rustic and robust dish is perfect for a snow day. It's simple and easy to pull together. Plan ahead, as you should marinate the rabbit for 24 hours. We serve it with polenta.

—Nick Strawhecker DANTE RISTORANTE PIZZERIA | OMAHA, NE

RABBIT

Hindquarters and forequarters of 1 rabbit

1 bottle Chianti Classico wine

1 tablespoon fennel seeds, toasted and ground

Salt and freshly ground black pepper, to taste

1 tablespoon olive oil, plus more as needed

1 tablespoon butter

12 whole cipollini onions, peeled

1½ heads garlic, cloves peeled and crushed

5 sprigs fresh thyme

4 stems fresh sage, with leaves

3 fresh bay leaves

4–6 cups chicken stock

POLENTA

2–2½ cups chicken stock, plus more as needed

1 cup heavy cream

½ cup white polenta

½ cup finely grated Grana Padano cheese

1 tablespoon olive oil, plus more to taste

Salt and freshly ground black pepper, to taste

SAUTÉED CARROTS AND TURNIPS

1 tablespoon butter

1 tablespoon olive oil

6 mini carrots, scrubbed

6 mini turnips, scrubbed

Salt and freshly ground black pepper, to taste

WHERE TO FIND…

Rabbit
Rabbit, Rabbit, Rabbit
Pickrell, NE

Herbs, Vegetables
Rhizosphere Farm
Missouri Valley, IA

TO MAKE THE RABBIT

Place the rabbit pieces in a nonreactive container and cover them with the wine. Make sure the pieces have room to move in the container and that they are completely submerged in the wine. (If you need a little more wine, open another bottle.) Cover the container and put it in the refrigerator for the rabbit pieces to marinate overnight.

The next day, remove the rabbit pieces from the wine, pat them dry with paper towels, and reserve the wine. Generously season the rabbit pieces on both sides with the ground fennel, salt, and pepper.

In a Dutch oven, heat the oil over medium–high heat. When the oil begins to smoke, add the butter. Sear the rabbit pieces well on both sides. Do not crowd the Dutch oven, and cook in batches if you need to. Once all of the rabbit pieces are seared, put them on a plate and set aside.

Preheat the oven to 475°F.

Continued

If the Dutch oven looks a little dry, add a touch more oil. Sear the onions on all sides, add the crushed garlic cloves, and sauté.

Tie the thyme sprigs and sage together in a bundle and add it to the Dutch oven along with the reserved wine and bay leaves. Scrape the bottom of the pan to pick up any brown bits. Bring the mixture to a rolling boil and reduce the liquid by ½. Once the liquid is reduced, remove from the heat and add the rabbit back to the Dutch oven. Pour enough of the stock over the rabbit pieces so they are completely submerged in the liquid. Cover the Dutch oven with aluminum foil and then the lid. Place in the oven and cook for 2 hours.

TO MAKE THE POLENTA

When the rabbit has about 20 minutes left to cook, combine the stock and heavy cream in a large saucepan and bring to a boil. Reduce the heat to low and very slowly pour in the polenta while whisking vigorously. You don't want lumpy polenta. Cook on low for about 45 minutes, stirring occasionally, until the polenta is soft and creamy. Add more stock as needed. When the polenta has finished cooking, remove from the heat and add the Grana Padano cheese and olive oil. Season to taste with the salt and pepper.

TO MAKE THE CARROTS AND TURNIPS AND ASSEMBLE THE DISH

When the rabbit has finished cooking, remove it from the Dutch oven and pour a ladleful of the braising liquid over it. Remove and discard the bundle of herbs. Pour the rest of the braising liquid into a saucepan and simmer until it thickens and has reduced by about ⅔. (If your lid wasn't quite tight, much of the liquid may have evaporated in the oven. If that's the case, there is no need to reduce.)

In small sauté pan, heat the butter and olive oil over medium–high heat. Add the carrots and turnips. Sauté for about 5 to 8 minutes, until the vegetables are blistered and crisp-tender. Season to taste with the salt and pepper.

To serve, spoon the polenta onto individual plates, add some of the rabbit pieces, and spoon the reduced braising liquid over the top. Garnish with some of the carrots and turnips. Serve.

Travis Dunekacke

FARMER TD NICHE PORK | ELK CREEK, NE |
WWW.FACEBOOK.COM/TRAVIS.DUNEKACKE

At dawn, steam rises from a watershed lake and remains suspended above the valley. Just before a hill crests and falls toward the lake, Travis Dunekacke's heritage hog farm, TD Niche Pork, rises to greet us. A 1990 Ford pickup, stuffed with leftover cider apples from nearby Kimmel Orchard and Arbor Day Farm, fills the air with the stench of sweet, rotting fruit.

Travis stands on the slope of his hog farm, twisting his hands and shifting his weight from one leg to the other while the photographer tries to capture his image. In the background, 200 umber, black, and red pigs frolic in their pens, rooting, eating apple sludge, and awaiting their final days before slaughter. As a farmer and a lover of good food, Travis built his brand on quality meat with exemplary fat and flavor. Top regional chefs and dedicated home cooks alike recognize the value of his Berkshire and Red Wattle hogs. He doesn't believe in cutting corners or sloppy work. He believes in creating meat that tastes exceptional.

After working in the large-scale commodity hog business for a number of years, he felt there was a better way to raise the animals. He

believed that, provided with the right opportunity, demand for the tender, moist meat of little-known heritage breeds would grow. He was right.

"As early as the 1930s, there were 35 breeds of pigs being raised on US farms. By the 1980s, it was down to five to eight breeds. Only three or four breeds are used in the commodity system today," Travis says. "[Heritage breeds] have been in our past, and for whatever reason they've been forgotten and then brought back. They just didn't fit into the post–World War II industrial commodity [food] system."

We walk the farm, amid the dust and snorts, as Travis explains the differentiating features of each pig: Red Wattle is exactly as it sounds, a red-haired pig with two long wattles below its jowls; Big Black has large, floppy, angel-wing ears; and the prized black-and-white Berkshire is valued for its marbling, which creates moist meat and lends itself well to cooking with high heat.

As a farmer and a lover of good food, Travis built his brand on quality meat with exemplary fat and flavor.

Commercial hog production is big business in the Plains states, but the model has changed considerably during the second half of the 20th century. According to the National Pork Producers Council, the United States boasts 67,000 pork operations today, compared with nearly 3 million in the 1950s. More than half of those farms produce more than 5,000 pigs per year. That makes TD Niche farm, with its 200 pigs, little bigger than a wide spot in the road—and Travis is just fine with that. Having a personal relationship with the chefs and people who buy his pork is a big part of his business plan.

He reaches into his truck and pulls out a plastic container full of smoked pork. He sets it on the fence post of a pigpen and hands me a square paper napkin.

"Here, you have to try this," he says, placing a heaping pile of shredded meat on my napkin. "It's what pork should taste like." And once again, he is right. ∎

Spice-Rubbed Slow-Cooker Pork

SERVES 4

During the winter, we rely more on local proteins (beef, pork, chicken, lamb) for our restaurant menu. I personally enjoy the ebb and flow that the seasons bring. It allows for diversity in our diet, and keeps the menu from getting stagnant by making the same old thing day after day.

Travis Dunekacke at TD Niche Pork (p. 191) specializes in heritage breeds and supplies our pork. We take delivery of two whole hogs every three weeks. Travis sends them to us as primal cuts, portioned into the main sections of shoulder, loin, belly, and ham. From there, we break them down further into the specific cuts we want to use. This recipe calls for pork shoulder, which is an excellent combination of fat and lean meat that responds well to slow cooking.

—*Kevin Shinn* BREAD AND CUP | LINCOLN, NE

1 16-ounce can diced mild green chilies (undrained)
1 yellow onion, finely diced
4 cloves garlic, finely minced
1 cup water
2 tablespoons brown sugar
2 teaspoons kosher salt
1 teaspoon pumpkin pie spice
1 teaspoon chile powder
1 teaspoon freshly ground black pepper
¼ teaspoon ground cayenne pepper
1 3–4-pound pork shoulder

WHERE TO FIND...

Pork
TD Niche Pork
Elk Creek, NE

In a slow cooker, combine the green chilies, onion, garlic, and water.

In a small bowl, mix the brown sugar and all the spices together until evenly blended. Rub the pork shoulder with the spice mixture and then place it in the slow cooker, on top of the green chile mixture. As the pork cooks, the spice rub will develop a nice, flavorful outer layer. Set the slow cooker on high for 6 to 7 hours. The pork is ready when it pulls apart easily with a fork.

Remove the meat from the slow cooker. Discard the cooking juice and chilies, or strain and freeze the broth for another day. Shred the pork with a fork for sandwiches, or serve sliced as a main course with mashed potatoes and gravy. Store any leftovers in the refrigerator for up to 1 week.

Dave Hutchinson

FARMER HUTCHINSON ORGANIC RANCH | ROSE, NE

We pile into a red Gator that is prone to overheating and drive into the bison herd. A family of sand-colored grouse pops up from the green-stemmed, red-tipped prairie grasses to find a resting place away from the rumbling engine. I have only seen a living bison one other time in my life, and it was much farther away than the hulking giants now before me.

The animals clearly see Dave Hutchinson, my driver and the owner of Hutchinson Organic Ranch, as a member of the herd—a leader, even. The brown- and rust-colored beasts surround us, their heads the size of half my body. Their presence is not intimidating, however; it is calming and serene. Some wallow in bogs created from the region's high water table, others tend to calves, but most of them just stand there and stare at us or quietly munch on little bluestem and Indian prairie grasses. Perhaps they have been blessed with an evolutionary peace of mind that comes from being the largest animal on the North American prairie, or maybe it is just the majesty of the entire 5,000-acre organic ranch that I was sensing.

One bison in particular seems skeptical of my presence. At 25, he is the eldest of the herd and has been at the ranch almost since its

inception. The herd is closed, meaning Dave doesn't bring in animals from outside breeders or other sources. Aside from the skeptic, all of his bison are born and bred and will eventually die on this prairie.

"You want to keep the great-great grandmothers and the great-great grandfathers around because they teach the calves how to be buffalo," explains Dave as he kneels in the pasture to pose for a photo. He goes on to discuss how feedlot buffalo don't know how to behave when given the chance to roam.

Dave didn't grow up ranching in these hills; rather, he was raised just outside of Lincoln, where his father worked as a state soil conservationist in the 1960s. Dave knew, however, that he always wanted to live and work in a place like this.

"We are caretakers of the bison, which means we manage the grass, the meadows, this prairie," he says.

We stand among them, listening as they tear away and chew the grasses, doing their part to keep the biodiversity of the plains in balance. When it's time to harvest the animals, Dave says those who are ready to die usually step forward. He calls to them, and they come.

"There was time when I thought, well, what if the wrong one steps forward, but you know what, it's always the right one," says Dave.

He restarts the Gator and we begin our multihour drive to the highest point on his land, leaving the bison to graze. As we climb in elevation,

small red orbs begin to appear at the base of the grasses. He stops, pulls out his knife, and slices the stems. He offers me the handful of rose hips.

"These are great for you, good in tea," says Dave, whose mother died of cancer at the age of 50. The experience influenced his passion for organic food and grass-fed, pastured meats. He doesn't shirk at expressing his disgust at feedlots, corn syrup, or immunizations, preferring instead to treat ailments with homeopathic remedies.

It is obvious he wants me to understand the value of these grasses. He stops again, jumps out, and hands me a few blades of prairie sandreed. "This," he says, holding the wheat-colored stalk up against the fading light, "helps to hold the hills in place." We continue as the sun begins to burn out, stopping for more grasses along the way, plucking strands of switchgrass, sand love grass, sage, and sideoats grama. We reach a hill he calls Pikes Peak. Natural lakes rest on either side of us, and I feel a true sense of how gentle and peaceful these grasslands are. We linger and watch the sun dip below a crested hill in the distance, then turn around and make our journey back to the home he shares with his wife, Sue.

When our final goodbyes are said, I walk down the wooden stairs of his porch to my car. My arms are wrapped around a prairie grass bouquet, a box of nutritional supplements, and a package of bison jerky. It seems like a fitting gift after spending nearly six hours exploring an organic bison ranch that's tucked into the gently rolling Sandhills of Nebraska, with a man who cares more about the land than most I've ever met. ■

Natural lakes rest on either side of us, and I feel a true sense of how gentle and peaceful these grasslands are.

Spaghetti Squash Carbonara

SERVES 6 (ABOUT 1½ CUPS PER PERSON)

Comfort food has always been my favorite style of food. I have never been a fan of dishes that take longer to say than they take to eat. This is a simple comfort food dish brought into the 21st century with spaghetti squash.

—George Formaro CENTRO | DES MOINES, IA

2 large spaghetti squash (about 4 pounds total)

10 slices bacon, chopped

1½ cups thinly sliced mushrooms (your favorite kind will do)

1 onion, sliced thin

2 cloves garlic, chopped

2 teaspoons salt, or to taste

1 teaspoon freshly ground black pepper, or to taste, plus more for garnish

1½ cups heavy cream

⅓ cup grated parmesan cheese, plus more for garnish

WHERE TO FIND...

Spaghetti Squash
Grade A Gardens
Johnston, IA

Garlic
Cleverley Farms
Mingo, IA

Preheat the oven to 350°F.

Halve the squash lengthwise. Scoop out and discard the seeds. Wrap the squash in aluminum foil and roast for about 1 hour, or until you can easily remove the flesh with a fork. While still warm, use a fork to scrape the flesh from the shells. Discard the shells and reserve the flesh.

In a large, deep sauté pan, cook the bacon. Remove it from the pan and drain on paper towels. Reserve 2 tablespoons of the fat in the pan and discard the rest or save it for another use.

Add the mushrooms and onion to the pan of bacon fat and cook over medium-high heat. Once the onion is softened, add the garlic and sauté for 1 more minute. Add the salt and pepper, then transfer the mixture to a bowl. Set the pan back over the heat, add the cream, and bring to a boil, letting the cream thicken slightly. This should take about 3 to 5 minutes. Fold the reserved squash flesh into the cream and cook until the squash is just reheated. Remove from the heat and stir in the bacon, cheese, and cooked onion and mushrooms. Garnish with more parmesan cheese and freshly ground pepper. Serve.

Roasted Capocollo with Cannellini Beans and Sautéed Red Cabbage

SERVES 6–8

Capocollo (or capicola) is pig's neck, traditionally cured for a couple of weeks and then slowly cooked. However, in this dish, we are using the shoulder. We'll cure it for a shorter period and roast it in the oven for a few hours. The spices provide warmth and heat, which balances the bitterness of the cabbage and the creaminess of the beans. In combination with a full table of family or friends, this dish is just what we need on the cold winter days when we're snowed in.

The cure time for the capocollo is five days, so I recommend starting this dish at the beginning of the week so it's ready for the weekend.

—*Bryce Coulton* THE FRENCH BULLDOG | OMAHA, NE

CAPOCOLLO

3 tablespoons kosher salt

2 tablespoons ground paprika

1 tablespoon ground cayenne pepper

1 tablespoon freshly ground black pepper

1 3-pound pork shoulder (also known as Boston butt or bone-out pork butt)

CANNELLINI BEANS

2 cups dried cannellini beans

¼ cup red wine vinegar

3 cloves garlic, crushed

4 sprigs fresh thyme

1 sprig fresh rosemary

½ cup olive oil

¼ teaspoon kosher salt, or to taste

TO MAKE THE CAPOCOLLO

In a small bowl, combine all the spices. Evenly coat the pork shoulder with the spice mixture. If your pork shoulder has butcher's twine or netting, remove it before rubbing the shoulder with the spice mixture. Place the spice-rubbed pork into a plastic bag, remove the air, and seal the bag. Place it into a container or on a plate and chill in the refrigerator for 5 days.

Preheat the oven to 350°F.

Remove the pork shoulder and rinse off the spices. Set the pork on a wire rack over a baking sheet. Let the meat sit at room temperature for 20 minutes.

Loosely cover the pork shoulder with aluminum foil and roast for 2½ to 3 hours, until the internal temperature of the pork reaches 135°F. Set aside, still covered, for 30 minutes. The carryover cooking will bring the internal temperature to 145°F. Keep warm until ready to serve.

TO MAKE THE BEANS

Pick through the beans to remove and discard any stones or debris. Rinse and drain the beans. Cover the beans with water and let soak overnight.

In a large saucepan, add the beans, the vinegar, the garlic, the thyme and rosemary sprigs, and enough water to cover the beans by 2 inches. Bring to a boil, then reduce to a simmer for about 1 hour, until the beans are softened but not mushy. Both the skin and the bean should be tender. Remove from the heat, drain, and discard the herb sprigs and crushed garlic cloves.

Transfer the beans to a serving bowl. Add the oil and salt and gently stir to coat. Keep warm until ready to serve.

SAUTÉED RED CABBAGE

2 teaspoons olive oil

1 medium onion, finely chopped

2 cloves garlic, finely chopped

½ large head red cabbage, chopped into ½-inch strips and crosscut into 2-inch strips (about 6 cups)

2 teaspoons fennel seeds

¾ teaspoon kosher salt, or to taste

WHERE TO FIND...

Pork
Truebridge Foods
Omaha, NE

Red Cabbage
Shadow Brook Farm
Lincoln, NE

TO MAKE THE CABBAGE

In a large saucepan, heat the oil over medium heat. Add the onion and sauté until softened, about 2 minutes. Add the garlic and sauté for about 1 more minute. Add the cabbage, fennel seeds, and salt and cook over low heat until the cabbage is crisp-tender, about 20 minutes. Transfer the cabbage to a serving dish and serve it along with the capocollo and beans.

Note: Do not add salt until the beans are completely cooked, as it causes them to harden.

Boozy Eggnog

MAKES 2½ QUARTS

When I lived in Colorado, a friend of mine hosted a party each December. A week before the event, he made at least five gallons of 'nog. When the celebration ended, he and his wife sent us all off with a quart-sized mason jar of their fantastic, creamy, boozy masterpiece. This recipe is my variation on the tradition started by these friends. Make this a week before you want to serve it. It will keep for at least three weeks in the refrigerator.

—*Michael Haskett* M.B. HASKETT DELICATESSEN | SIOUX FALLS, SD

6 eggs

¾ cup honey

1½ cups whiskey, divided

3½ cups heavy cream, divided

2 cups whole milk

1 cup dark rum

½ cup Frangelico

2 teaspoons freshly ground
    nutmeg, plus more for garnish

1 healthy pinch sea salt

2 tablespoons granulated sugar

1 teaspoon vanilla extract

Ground cinnamon, for garnish

WHERE TO FIND...

Eggs
Berrybrook Organics
Marion, SD

Separate the yolks and the whites of the eggs. Place the yolks into a 5-quart bowl. Place the whites in a jar, seal the jar, and let chill in the refrigerator.

Whisk the yolks until they are creamy and thick, like pudding.

In a small saucepan over low heat, slightly warm the honey, just so it pours easily. Slowly add the honey to the yolks, while whisking continuously. Add ¾ cup of the whiskey and whisk to combine. Chill the mixture in the refrigerator for 1 hour. After 1 hour, remove from the refrigerator.

In a medium bowl, or in the bowl of a stand mixer fitted with the whisk attachment, whip 1¼ cups of the cream until soft peaks form. Fold the whipped cream into the yolk mixture. Add the milk, remaining whiskey, dark rum, Frangelico, nutmeg, and salt. Refrigerate overnight, alongside the jar of egg whites.

The next day, in a medium bowl, or in the bowl of a stand mixer fitted with the whisk attachment, whip another 1¼ cups of the cream into soft peaks. Set aside.

In another bowl, or in the washed bowl of a stand mixer fitted with the whisk attachment, whip the egg whites until they form medium peaks. Fold the whites into the whipped cream in thirds, then fold that mixture into the yolk mixture in thirds. At this point, you can store the eggnog in clean, sealed containers in the refrigerator for up to 3 weeks.

The eggnog will separate over time; just before serving, pour it into the bowl of a stand mixer fitted with the whisk attachment and whip for about 3 minutes or so. Pour the eggnog into a punch bowl.

Whip the remaining 1 cup of the cream with the sugar and vanilla extract until soft peaks form. You can fold the sweetened whipped cream directly into the eggnog, or place a dollop on top of each individual glass of 'nog. Garnish with a dusting of nutmeg and cinnamon. Serve.

Sean Wilson

CHEF PROOF | 1301 LOCUST ST. | DES MOINES, IA | 515.244.0655 | PROOFRESTAURANT.COM

W hite ceiling fans like those found on front porches in sleepy Southern towns circle slowly overhead in the dining room at Proof, a 14-table restaurant on the corner of 13th and Locust in Des Moines. Beneath the fans each table of four waits patiently to greet the lunch crowd with a single yellow plume of goldenrod resting in a simple white vase.

It's 10 a.m. and chef Sean Wilson readies himself for a weekly meeting with four key staff members. His baseball cap with a patch that says *Make Cornbread Not War* and a navy pullover windbreaker contribute to his youthful appearance. He places a yellow legal pad on the black table and begins to discuss the successes and failures of the past week. Each member contributes to the sometimes intense conversation, and it's obvious all are driving toward the same goal: perfection.

Sean finishes his meeting, walks over, and introduces himself to me. A bracelet made from the friar's ropes of Frangelico bottles offsets his gold wedding band. He talks about saving tables, hosting, and the importance of perfectly executed hospitality.

While his food, rich with Mediterranean influence, is stylistically stunning and unequivocally creative, his approach is pretty down to earth. When he was growing up in a self-described "weird" Irish–Italian–Filipino family, with 27 first cousins, food was everywhere—and his maternal grandfather was at the heart of it.

"In my family, food was the catalyst that brought everything and everyone together, but it was never the be-all end-all," Sean says over coffee. "I remember going home for a visit once and seeing the whole family, all of these people together, and my grandfather was standing at the head of the table. They were all eating, but they were all there because of that one man. What he created through food, not the food itself, is what brought us together."

Though hours at the table and his grandfather's culinary traditions were the foundation upon which Sean's career as a chef was built, he first followed another familial path, as a third-generation member of the

RECIPES FROM SEAN:

› Beet Salad with Goat Cheese Cream and Passion Fruit Marshmallow (p. 50)
› Tomato Chutney (p. 91)
› Spicy Brussels Sprouts (p. 122)
› Goat Cheese Sorbet with Peanut Brittle Cookies (p. 214)

US Coast Guard. It was only after his military service that he attended culinary school in Montpelier, Vermont, where he met his wife, a Des Moines native. After traveling a bit, they moved to Iowa for her career in publishing. Sean worked at various restaurants in town before he found the perfect home at Proof.

He and his business partner, Zachary Mannheimer, purchased the restaurant in 2012, and within a year Sean was a semifinalist for the James Beard Award Best Chef: Midwest.

"When we decided to move, I thought, 'I'm moving to Des Moines, Iowa. The black earth of the United States; I'm going to be able to get everything,' but it was actually really hard to source locally at first," says Sean, who typically works with between three and five farmers to get enough of a certain product, such as tomatoes or greens. "The other thing is, just because it's local doesn't mean it's good. It has to be both."

For Sean the perfect dining experience comes from finding farmers who are truly passionate about their life's work and treating guests like long-lost friends. Food is extraordinary when savored slowly over a conversation among those who pull up a chair and enjoy each other's company with little more than an exceptional meal, a good drink, and a plume of goldenrod between them. ∎

Food is extraordinary when savored slowly over a conversation among those who pull up a chair and enjoy each other's company with little more than an exceptional meal, a good drink, and a plume of goldenrod between them.

Goat Cheese Sorbet with Peanut Brittle Cookies

SERVES 6 (½ CUP OF SORBET AND 2 COOKIES PER PERSON)

This lovely and light sorbet pairs the soft brightness of lemon with the tangy creaminess of goat cheese. The sweet crunch of the brittle cookies is the perfect accompaniment.

    The sorbet mixture has to chill for four hours before you churn it in an ice cream maker, so plan ahead.

—*Sean Wilson* PROOF | DES MOINES, IA

SIMPLE SYRUP

1½ cups water

1½ cups granulated sugar

SORBET

1 cup goat cheese

½ cup sour cream

½ cup heavy cream

2 cups Simple Syrup

1 lemon, for juicing and zesting

Pinch salt

COOKIES

¾ cup granulated sugar

¼ cup honey

3 tablespoons water

1 cup roasted, salted peanuts
    (skins removed)

2 tablespoons unsalted butter

¼ teaspoon baking soda

WHERE TO FIND...

Goat Cheese
Reichert's Dairy Air
Knoxville, IA

Honey
Ebert Honey Company
Lynnville, IA

TO MAKE THE SIMPLE SYRUP

In a small saucepan over medium heat, heat the water and sugar. Once the sugar dissolves, bring the mixture to a boil. Remove from the heat.

TO MAKE THE SORBET

In a large bowl, combine the goat cheese, sour cream, and heavy cream. Set aside.

Pour the 2 cups of still-warm simple syrup over the goat cheese mixture. Whisk until smooth.

Zest the entire lemon; reserve the zest for garnish. Juice ½ of the lemon and add the juice to the mixture, along with the salt. Whisk to incorporate. Cover the mixture and chill it in the refrigerator for at least 4 hours. Once the goat cheese mixture has finished chilling, spin the mixture in an ice cream maker, following the manufacturer's directions. Transfer to the freezer until ready to serve.

TO MAKE THE COOKIES

Line a baking sheet with parchment paper. Set aside.

In a large saucepan over medium heat, add the sugar, honey, and water, stirring occasionally, until the mixture reads 300°F on a candy thermometer. Remove from the heat and stir in the peanuts, butter, and baking soda. Working quickly, pour the mixture onto the prepared baking sheet. Use an oiled spatula to smooth the brittle out as much as possible.

Preheat the oven to 350°F.

When the brittle is cool to the touch and cracks easily, place it in a food processor. Reserve the baking sheet lined with parchment paper. Pulse the brittle until a powder is formed.

Pour the powder in a thin layer onto the reserved baking sheet and bake until it bubbles, darkens a bit, and forms a thin sheet, about 8 to 10 minutes. Remove from the oven and let cool for about 1 minute.

Pull the parchment with the brittle off of the baking sheet and onto a cutting board or other surface safe for cutting. Using a pizza cutter or knife, cut the still-warm brittle into wide strips, then squares, then triangles. Gently lift each triangle from the parchment and lay on a flat surface to finish cooling, or lay across a rolling pin to form a slight curve. If the brittle firms up before you cut and form all the cookies, just put it back in the oven for 30 to 45 seconds to let it soften again.

To serve, measure ½ cup of the sorbet into each bowl. Garnish with 2 cookies and some of the lemon zest.

Acknowledgments

In many ways, this book was written on the strength of my husband's back. It would be easy to sum up my gratitude and appreciation by saying that you, Steve Widhalm, supported me, but what you did wasn't easy and the word support doesn't properly define your actions. You looked at me, pregnant with our second child, and told me it was a perfect time to write a book, when it wasn't. You honored the wedding vows you wrote nearly a decade earlier when you promised to support my goals as a professional and my dreams of becoming a mother. You listened to me go on endlessly about the value of a home-cooked meal, farming issues, local food issues, and "cute little places" I wanted to check out. You worked hard at your own job, then came home and worked harder at being a good husband and father. You took the kids away for weekends, read drafts, and ate meals that had no resemblance to sloppy joes, grass fed or otherwise. You tolerated my nightly retreats to my office, my endless hours at the computer after the kids went to sleep, a kitchen in constant shambles, and my epic road trips. Above all, you never complained. Not once. You are the kind of man strong families are built on. I'm pretty amazed by you, but then again, I always have been. Thanks for all of it. I love you dearly.

The joys of my life, Jackson and Juniper, motivate me to not only notice but to also absorb the spectacular beauty that surrounds us. You have accompanied me on most, if not all, of the farmers' market visits, CSA pickups, farm tours, restaurant experiences, and specialty shop and grocery trips for this book—sometimes willingly, while eating broccoli branches like snow cones; other times, I'm sure you would've preferred to zoom cars across the floor or colored ponies at the kitchen table. You are both too little to understand how amazing you've been through it all, but, just so it's on record, you were fantastic little helpers and I'm so proud of you. I love you.

I have been wholeheartedly amazed by the kindness and generosity of the farmers, chefs, and artisans featured in this book. They gave of their time and talents without any promise that their recipes or stories would come to fruition. That kind of willingness to help others without a reward or an IOU is, I think, a special component of this region.

Thank you to all who contributed to this book and my own food journey, but especially to Clayton Chapman, who was the first chef to commit to this project. He endured endless questions from me and always responded with grace. To Bryce Coulton, who became a great source of inspiration and guidance as I was finishing the manuscript, and, of course, for the apple cake. Both Bryce and Travis Dunekacke became my source for all things related to and resembling pork; their knowledge and willingness to share it made this book better. Thank you to Krista Dittman and Rufus Musser III, who sent Dana Damewood and me on the road with oodles of their delicious cheese, half of which was eaten right in the car. There were many chefs, farmers, and artisans who intentionally took the time to serve us food during our 15- to 17-hour road trips, including Kevin Shinn, whose simple corn on the cob and sliced tomatoes will go down in history as one of my favorite meals—it was 10 a.m. and we were already six hours into our day. To the wonderful John Hamburger, who wouldn't let us leave with fewer than 15 loaves of his delicious bread. He is, above all things, a really nice guy. To Maggie Pleskac for packing up lovely strawberry muffins. To Dave Hutchinson, who spent the day showing my entire family some of the most beautiful land in Nebraska, and to his wife, Sue, for dinner. To George and Karen Johnson, for inviting my family, children and all, into their home and feeding us, but especially for getting the John Deere pedal car out of the garage attic for my son to drive. To Kristine Moberg and Mitch Jackson at Queen City Bakery for the cookies, the lemon marshmallows, and the deliciously unforgettable fig–goat cheese turnover. To Brian O'Malley and Taryn Huebner for serving as a resource for questions about fat, and temperature, and life in general.

Many of the stories within these pages first appeared, in some form, in the *Reader*, *Edible Omaha*, and *Nebraska Life Magazine*. Thank you for allowing me to reprint them. To John Heaston, my publisher at the *Reader* and my dear friend: thanks for teaching me everything you know. I'm a better writer because of your tutelage. To Krista O'Malley, my editor at the *Reader*: thank you for allowing me to step away from my responsibilities as a columnist to write this book. To Amy Brown, editor and copublisher, and Lucy Wilson, my publisher at *Edible Omaha*: I'm sorry I missed nearly every deadline once the book started. Thanks for not replacing me, for continuing to offer growth opportunities, and for being the type of employers who respect and support women with families. To Christopher Amundson, my publisher at *Nebraska Life Magazine*: thank you for my many movable deadlines. Your flexibility was an essential component of this project.

To Dana Damewood for signing onto a project without knowing its future, for providing valuable road trip conversations, and, this goes without saying, for your amazing skills behind a camera. To Ying Ruan and Jackie Sterba, thank you for your beautiful prop and food styling. To Laurie Owens at The Whistle Stop Country Store in Elkhorn, Nebraska, thank you for lending me so many dishes, napkins, and random accessories on a handshake.

To the entire team at Agate Publishing for recognizing the potential of the Great Plains states and their culinary repertoire, I thank you and I deeply value your investment not only in me, but in all the people featured in this book. Thanks to Doug Seibold for taking a chance on me, to Danielle McLimore for your patience and guidance, to Morgan Krehbiel for the beautiful design, and to Eileen Johnson for being an early champion of the book.

To the encouragers, the rays of sunshine, and the bringers of hope, Cindy Driscoll, Shannon Hervieux, Bruce Hugunin, Meghan Malik, Sheryl Houston, Sunshine Bliss, Terri Storm, Denae Mayfield, Wendy Pella, Alexis LaGuardia Studenberg, and Crystal Johnson: I adore you all. Cindy helped me chop, cook, test, clean, and stuff, but most of all, she kept me going through her relentless optimism when I thought I was going to be sucked under. I could not have done this without her. Shannon, Denae, Alexis, and Wendy tested recipes, sampled recipes, and gave me great feedback and lots of encouragement on life, motherhood, and food. Meghan, Terri, and Sunshine, thank you for providing the much-needed moral support, long walks, and glasses of wine, sometimes at the same time. To Sheryl Houston for telling me about Back Alley Bakery. To Alison Bickel, thank you for your kindness, friendship, collaborative approach, and guidance—you are a rare gem. Finally, thanks so much to Crystal Johnson, who cheered me on to the finish line and then handed me a cupcake.

To Michelle Cartwright-Bruckner at Harp & Squirrel, thanks for your awesome attitude and your willingness to take on any project and do whatever needs to be done. Danelle Myer is an inspiration to women everywhere, but especially to women who farm and women who write about them. Thank you to Ellie Archer for being a wonderful friend and mentor.

At various points throughout the writing and researching of this book, I reached out Kristine Gerber, Timothy Schaffert, Jonathan Segura, Ivy Manning, Isa Chandra Moskowitz, Sally Ekus, Elizabeth Evans, Rod Colvin, John T. Price, Steve Semken, Angela Glover, and Kyle Tonniges. Each offered his or her own bit of expertise and guidance. They provided invaluable feedback on drafts, proposals, research, and organization. All were generous with their knowledge and time, and for that I am forever grateful. Your insight prevented many stumbles.

I tested each recipe in the book at least three times, often many more. I also sent some recipes out to an amazing group of home cooks who provided invaluable feedback about cooking times, temperature, and instructions. All spent time and energy helping me make the recipes perfect. In addition to those I have already mentioned, thank you to: Debra Kusleika, Janelle Shank, Keith T. Dubes, Kara Schweiss, Nancy Conley, and Esperonsa McGee. Ann Rourke, thanks for testing, but also thanks for being one of the most amazing, kind-hearted, and joyful people I have ever known.

To Donna and Randy Mehlin for taste-testing and for the continuous supply of cherries, and to Dawna Mowrey for the endless supply of eggs, moral support, and impromptu sharing of green beans. To Amy Barnett of Capra Fera Farm in Omaha, Nebraska, for her flexibility and food-growing talent, and for meeting me in a parking lot with her beautiful and delicious sunchokes.

To the Nebraska Sustainable Agriculture Society; the Omaha Farmers Market; the Women, Food and Agriculture Network; the Practical Farmers of Iowa; and Amy Yaroch, who helped spread the word about the project while it was in its infancy. A special thanks to William Powers, Bahia Nightengale, Heidi Walz, and Lori Tatreau, who offered support and were wellsprings of knowledge and connections.

There were many times during this process when I was nomadic and requested quiet places to write. A special thanks to Barb Balok and John Fruhwirth for both opening your home to me and testing some of the more complicated recipes, but especially because Barb has been propelling me forward since the day we met. To Joi and Colin Brown, for giving me office space and feeding me while I took over your desk, and for 1,000 other things. To the Minne Lusa Ladies, Beth Richards and Sharon Olson, you have become dear friends and I can't thank you enough for the joy and generosity you dole out to everyone you meet. Thank you so much for the time and space you shared with me. To Jim Trebbien for offering the extra space in his home, but also for running a wonderful culinary arts program at Metropolitan Community College that supports budding chefs and home cooks alike.

As a part-time, work-from-home mom with a project, I needed lots of help in the form of child care. A special thanks goes out to Donna Widhalm, Ken and Coletta Widhalm, Jennifer VanCleve, and Deb Schuiteman, who did the most important job of all by providing a fun, loving, and safe environment for my children while I cooked, cleaned, interviewed, researched, and wrote. A special thanks to Stephanie Varilek and Inessa Wilcox and Deb for letting me know when spots opened and time allowed, but also for the times I changed my mind, canceled altogether, and rearranged dates. Not only were you caring in your responses, but you actually celebrated the days I canceled to spend time cuddling on the couch and watching *Curious George* with the kids.

To my maternal grandmother, Rita Price, you are a beacon of determination, creative drive, and curiosity. Thank you for putting a pen and steno pad in my hand as a child and telling me to write about what I saw flying by me through the car window. To my paternal grandmother, Barbara Miller, thank you for teaching me about hard work, dedication, and grit. To my grandfather, James Miller, thank you for teaching me about the importance of an education as we sat in the front seat of the car when I was seven years old. To my dad, Mike Miller, thank you for teaching me to get up every time I fell, for always being there for me, and for being passionate about dinner. To Sheila Foresman, my mom and relentless cheerleader, food taster, and gardener extraordinaire, thanks for teaching me the value of working in the dirt. That simple gift has given me so much joy. To my brother Aaron and his wife, Sarah, thanks for eating my food, good or bad, for years; I'm so glad we are close. To my brother Ryan, thanks for being fearless. You have no idea how much that part of you inspires me. To my brother Ethan, thanks for being one of the kindest, most loving people I have ever met. You are a constant reminder of the good in the world. To my sister Stephanie, thank you for doing the dishes, chopping the vegetables, stirring the sauces, letting me constantly stuff your face, and being a wonderful aunt to your niece and nephew. Without your help, I couldn't have finished the book and that is no exaggeration. To my sister Emily, I love you and I miss you dearly; feeding you was my greatest pleasure.

If I did not mention you by name, please know you remain in my heart and I am full of gratitude for all of you.

References

"Dairy Economics in Nebraska: An Analysis of Costs and Returns and Comparisons with Other States." http://digitalcommons.unl.edu/cgi/viewcontent.cgi?article=1519&context=extensionhist

"Dairy in the Midwest." www.midwestdairy.com/0t253p205/dairy-in-the-midwest.

David Kamp. *The United States of Arugula: How We Became a Gourmet Nation.* New York: Broadway Books, 2006.

Deborah Krasner. *Good Meat: The Complete Guide to Sourcing and Cooking Sustainable Meat.* New York: Stewart, Tabori and Chang, 2010.

"Freezing Eggs." www.incredibleegg.org/egg-facts/eggcyclopedia/f/freezing-eggs.

"Homemade Eggnog Can Kill Salmonella with Booze." http://abcnews.go.com/Health/holiday-miracle-homemade-eggnog-kills-salmonella-booze/story?id=17905639.

"Pork Facts." www.nppc.org/pork-facts.

"Storage Times for the Refrigerator and Freezer." www.foodsafety.gov/keep/charts/storagetimes.html

Resources

Farmers and Artisans

Farm visits are by appointment only.

Iowa

Anything But Green Gardens
(p. 112)
Vinton, IA
319.453.8303
anythingbutgreengardens@hotmail.com
mushrooms

Blooms Organic (p. 43, 47, 71, 116)
Crescent, IA
402.639.7365
rebecca_bloom@hotmail.com
produce

Butcher Crick Farms (p. 91, 122)
Carlisle, IA
515.720.6969
www.facebook.com/pages/Butcher-
Crick-Farms/296187926923
tomatoes

Cleverley Farms (p. 20, 27, 66, 74,
146, *147*, 152, 204)
Mingo, IA
515.778.6202
www.facebook.com/CleverleyFarms
produce

DeBruin Brothers (p. 152)
Oskaloosa, IA
641.673.5022
www.debruinbrothers.com
rabbit

Double K Farms (p. 90)
Clarinda, IA
402.516.2062
www.doublekfarms.com
produce, eggs

Ebert Honey Company (p. 214)
Lynnville, IA
641.527.2639
www.eberthoney.com
honey

Grade A Gardens (p. 51, 91, 204)
Johnston, IA
515.554.4306
www.gradeagardens.com
produce

Grimes Sweet Corn (p. 74)
Granger, IA
515.986.3437
www.grimessweetcorn.com
corn

Honey Creek Farms (p. 47, 181)
Oakland, IA
402.819.8304
neverendingharvest.com
produce

Kroul Farms (p. 39, 175)
Mount Vernon, IA
319.895.8944
www.kroulfarms.com
produce, eggs

La Quercia (p. 142, 171, 175)
Norwalk, IA
515.981.1625
laquercia.us
cured meats

Majinola Meats (p. 181)
Panama, IA
866.609.MEAT
www.majinolameats.com
beef

Maxwell Farms (p. 186)
State Center, IA
515.460.2705
maxwellfarms02@gmail.com
produce

Milton Creamery (p. *17*, 20, 146)
Milton, IA
641.656.4094
www.miltoncreamery.com
cow's milk cheese

Niman Ranch (p. 20, 74)
www.nimanranch.com

Niman Ranch is headquartered in Alameda,
California. It is a national company that
works with family farmers and ranchers
who raise livestock humanely, without
hormones or antibiotics. The organization
expanded in 1995 after partnering with
Paul Willis, from Thornton, Iowa. He still
oversees the hog operation in Iowa. Thornton is the founder of the Niman Ranch Pork
Company, a subsidiary of Niman Ranch,
which was founded by Bill Niman, who is
no longer with the company, in the 1970s.
More than half of the 700 single-family
farms in the Niman Ranch network are in
Nebraska, Iowa, and South Dakota.

Pavelka's Point Meats (p. 39)
Mount Vernon, IA
319-624-2392
loisbill@southslope.net
meat

Reichert's Dairy Air (p. 51, 214)
Knoxville, IA
641.218.4296
www.reichertsdairyair.com
goat cheese

Rhizosphere Farm (p. 30, *33*, 35, 90,
***123*, 130, 142, 181, 189)**
Missiouri Valley, IA
721.310.3715
402.310.3715
rhizospherefarm.org
produce, honey, eggs

Small's Fruit Farm (p. 136, *139*)
Mondamin, IA
712.646.2723
smallsfruitfarm.com
fruit

TableTop Farm (p. 51, 122)
Nevada, IA
515.291.8727
www.tabletopfarm.com
produce

The Cornucopia (p. 14, 100, *159*, 163)
Sioux Center, IA
712.490.8218
thecornucopiacsa.com
produce

Wild Woods Farm (p. 77, 175, *177*)
Solon, IA
319.333.2980
wildwoodscsa.com
produce

Kansas

Bainter Sunflower Oil (p. 63)
Hoxie, KS
785.675.2173
www.baintersunfloweroil.com
oil

Nebraska

26th Street Farm (p. 25, 67)
Hastings, NE
402.705.1664
produce

Branched Oak Farm (p. 33, 90, *95*, 97)
Raymond, NE
402.783.2124
branchedoakfarm.com
cow's milk cheese

Burbach's Countryside Dairy
(p. 14, 90, 100, 163, 181)
Hartington, NE
402.283.4625
burbachscountrysidedairy.com
milk, cheese

Clear Creek Organic Farms (p. 170)
Spalding, NE
308.750.1086
www.clearcreekorganicfarms.webs.com
butter, cheese, ice cream, beef, pork

Common Good Farm
(p. 24, *63*, 157, 182)
Raymond, NE
402.783.9005
www.commongoodfarm.com
produce, pork, beef, eggs

Community CROPS (p. 24, 227)
Lincoln, NE
402.474.9802
www.communitycrops.org
multifarm CSA

Donna Faimon (p. 170)
Lawrence, NE
402.756.7049
rdfaimon@gtmc.net
eggs

**Dutch Girl Creamery at Shadow
Brook Farm** (p. 43, *85*)
Lincoln, NE
402.421.2383
www.shadowbrk.com
goat cheese

Fehringer Farms (p. 63)
Sydney, NE
308.254.3330
www.fehringerfarms.com
grains, flour

George Paul Vinegar
(p. 8, 47, *133*, 136, 181)
Cody, NE
402.823.4067
www.georgepaulvinegar.com
vinegar

Grain Place Foods
(p. *60*, 90, 110)
Marquette, NE
888.714.7246
grainplacefoods.com
grains, flour, beans

Harvest Home (p. 22, 24, 157)
Waverly, NE
402.786.3476
harvesthomefarm.net
produce, honey

Heartland Nuts 'N More (p. 63, 182)
Valparaiso, NE
402.784.6887
www.heartlandnutsnmore.com
nuts

Hutchinson Organic Ranch (p. 197)
Rose, NE
402.273.4574
buffalo@nntc.net
bison

Marlene's Tortilleria (p. 157)
Lincoln, NE
402.438.9419
tortillas

Martin's Hillside Orchard (p. 157)
Ceresco, NE
402.665.2140
www.hillside-orchard.com
fruit

Naber's Produce (p. 99)
York, NE
402.728.5565
mail@nabersproducefarm.com
www.nabersproducefarm.com
produce

Plum Creek Farms (p. 35)
Burchard, NE
402.696.4535
plumcreekfarmsinc.com
chicken

Prairieland Dairy (p. 63)
Firth, NE
402.791.2228
www.prairielanddairy.com
milk

Rabbit, Rabbit, Rabbit (p. 189)
Pickrell, NE
402.239.0821
rabbit

Robinette Farms (p. 182)
Martell, NE
402.794.4025
www.robinettefarms.com
produce, eggs

Sanders Specialty Meats and Produce (p. 16, 121, 136)
Dwight, NE
402.545.2229
www.facebook.com/pages
/Sanders-Specialty-Meats-and
-Produce/126221260784807
produce, meat, honey

Shadow Brook Farm (p. 24, 59, 71, 85, 90, 136, 157, 171, 207)
Lincoln, NE
402.421.2383
www.shadowbrk.com
produce

Squeaky Green Organics (p. 43, 71, 99, 116)
Omaha, NE
402.575.7988
www.squeakygreenorganics.com
produce

TD Niche Pork (p. 191, 196)
Elk Creek, NE
402.335.0197
tdpork@gmail.com
www.facebook.com/travis.dunekacke
pork

Truebridge Foods (p. 30, 59, 130, 207)
1209 Harney St. Suite 300
Omaha, NE 68102
218.464.6944
www.truebridgefoods.com
pork

Walnut Creek Organic Ranch (p. 110)
Deweese, NE
402.200.0792
www.facebook.com/pages
/Walnut-Creek-Organic
-Ranch/297631213614429
beef, honey

South Dakota

Berrybrook Organics (p. 52, 208)
Marion, SD
605.925.7038
www.berrybrookorganics.com
berries, beef, eggs

Dakota Harvest Farm (p. 47)
Jefferson, SD
605.966.5490
www.dakotaharvestfarm.com
lamb

Deep Creek Honey (p. 167)
Hartford, SD
605.526.6780
deepcreekhoney@hotmail.com
www.facebook.com/deep.c.farm
honey

Linda's Gardens (p. 52, 81, 161)
Chester, SD
605.489.2651
www.lindasgardens.com
produce

Prairie Coteau Farm (p. 81, 161)
Astoria, SD
605.832.2062
www.prairiegarlic.com
garlic

Wild Idea Buffalo Co. (p. 161)
1575 Valley Dr.
Rapid City, SD 57703
866.658.6137
wildideabuffalo.com
bison

Restaurants

Iowa

Alba (p. 27, 66, 152, *185*)
524 E. 6th St.
Des Moines, IA 50309
515.244.0261
www.albadsm.com

Big Grove Brewery
(p. *39*, 77, 112, *172*, 174)
101 W. Main St.
Solon, IA 52333
319.624.2337
www.biggrovebrewery.com

Centro (p. 20, *73*, 74, 145, 204)
1003 Locust St.
Des Moines, IA 50309
515.248.1780
www.centrodesmoines.com

Proof (p. 50, 91, 122, *211*, 214)
1301 Locust St.
Des Moines, IA 50309
515.244.0655
proofrestaurant.com

Nebraska

Back Alley Bakery
(p. 25, 67, *105*, 110, 170, 222)
609 W. 2nd St.
Hastings, NE 68901
402.460.5056
www.backalleybakery.com

Bread and Cup
(p. 16, 99, *119*, 121, 196)
440 N. 8th St., Suite 150
Lincoln, NE 68508
402.438.2255
breadandcup.com

Dante Ristorante Pizzeria
(p. *33*, 35, 97, 141, 189)
16901 Wright Plaza
Omaha, NE 68130
402.932.3078
www.dantepizzeria.com

Maggie's Vegetarian Café (p. 3, *22*)
311 N. 8th St.
Lincoln, NE 68508
402.477.3959
maggiesvegetarian.com

The Boiler Room
(p. 43, *68*, 71, 116, 171)
1110 Jones St.
Omaha, NE 68102
402.916.9274
www.boilerroomomaha.com

The French Bulldog
(p. *28*, 30, 58, 126, 129, 206)
5003 Underwood Ave.
Omaha, NE 68132
402.505.4633
frenchbulldogomaha.com

The Grey Plume
(p. 3, *45*, 89, 126, 136, 180)
220 S. 31st Ave., Suite 3101
Omaha, NE 68131
402.763.4447
www.thegreyplume.com

South Dakota

M.B. Haskett Delicatessen
(p. 52, *78*, 80, 161, 208)
324 S. Phillips Ave.
Sioux Falls, SD 57104
605.367.1100
mbhaskett.com

Queen City Bakery
(p. 14, 100, 162, 167, *168*, 220)
324 E. 8th St.
Sioux Falls, SD 57103
605.274.6060
www.queencitybakery.com

Recipes by Type of Dish

Index

About the Author

Summer Miller is a freelance journalist whose work has appeared in *Saveur*, *Every Day with Rachael Ray*, *Edible Omaha*, *Edible Feast*, *Nebraska Life*, *Omaha Magazine*, and the *Reader*. She lives with her husband and two children just outside the fringes of Omaha, Nebraska where she spends most of her time thinking and writing about food. She blogs at www.scaldedmilk.com.

About the Photographer

Dana Damewood received her bachelor of fine art degree in photography from the Savannah College of Art and Design in 2003, where she was trained in all photographic mediums and processes. Her recognized work has been in fine art portraiture, in which she is skilled at capturing and reflecting life's important moments. She has shown her work at several galleries and has an established clientele base. Currently, Dana lives in Omaha, Nebraska, where she owns a portrait and wedding business. She also remains true to her fine art photography and has gallery exhibitions regularly.